SECOND EDITION
CIVIL LIABILITY IN CRIMINAL *Justice*

H.E. BARRINEAU III
University of South Carolina

anderson publishing co.
p.o. box 1576
cincinnati, oh 45201-1576
513-421-4142

Civil Liability in Criminal Justice, Second Edition

Copyright © 1994, 1987 by Anderson Publishing Co./Cincinnati, OH

All rights reserved. No part of this book may be reproduced in any form or by any electronic or mechanical means, including information storage and retrieval systems, without permission in writing from the publisher.

ISBN 0-87084-095-9
Library of Congress Catalog Number 93-74613

 The text of this book is printed on recycled paper.

Elisabeth Roszmann *Project Editor*   *Managing Editor* Kelly Humble

                                            Cover design by Vicki Shell

Introduction

In recent years there has been a dramatic increase in the number of lawsuits alleging misconduct on the part of criminal justice practitioners. More and more of these cases are now being filed in the federal courts, although such suits continue to be filed in state courts as well. The increase in civil liability suits against criminal justice practitioners has profound implications for individual practitioners as well as their employing agencies.

Criminal justice practitioners will, no doubt, continue to be sued because of the nature of their jobs. Law enforcement personnel place individuals in custody and often utilize force, sometimes deadly force, in performing their duties. Jail and correctional personnel impose limits on an individual's freedom of movement, and probation and parole agents also exercise considerable control over the lives of their clients. Thus, if an individual feels that his or her treatment by a criminal justice practitioner has been improper, a lawsuit often results. Such lawsuits are generally considered an "occupational hazard" by most criminal justice practitioners.

Although most criminal justice practitioners have a vague notion that they can be sued, few have any real understanding of their potential civil liability. Civil liability is complex and varies from jurisdiction to jurisdiction. Developments in the federal law have greatly expanded the scope of liability, and today local government units can be held liable for the conduct of police officers and jail personnel. Likewise, sheriffs, police chiefs, and mid-level supervisors can be held *personally* liable for the conduct of their subordinates; non-purposeful acts amounting to negligence can now be the basis for such lawsuits.

The purposes of this handbook are to expose the reader to civil liability generally and to the federal law specifically; to make the reader aware of the liability risks of criminal justice practitioners; and to indicate the proactive steps that can be taken to minimize the liability risks to practitioners and their employing agencies.

The first several chapters discuss the differences between criminal law and civil law, as well as defining the three categories of civil actions (or tort actions) that cover most of the lawsuits against criminal justice practitioners. How these general principles are applied in lawsuits against criminal justice personnel is discussed, as well as the major differences between state suits and federal suits. The revival of the 1871 federal legislation under which many civil liability actions against criminal justice personnel are now filed, and the payment of attorney's fees in those cases, are also discussed.

There are chapters discussing cases brought against practitioners, administrators and supervisors, and agencies in the criminal justice system. It must be noted that placing each group in separate chapters has been done for ease in comparing cases and issues, but the principles, interpretations, and concepts that arise in these cases are generally applicable to all components in the system. A concept or liability theory or interpretation that was developed in a case arising from the actions of a correctional officer can also be utilized to establish liability for a law enforcement officer in a future case. Therefore, the cases presented about one segment of the criminal justice system are just as applicable to actions in all other segments as well.

There are some viable defenses available to criminal justice practitioners and agencies when they find themselves named as defendants in a civil liability case. However, other than disproving factually that the events complained of did not occur, the defenses are rather limited, are not automatic, and must be proven to the satisfaction of a judge or jury. Therefore, prevention (avoiding the lawsuit in the first place) is a better strategy to undertake. This handbook presents some of the defenses and lawsuit prevention strategies available.

The case summaries presented in this handbook are in most cases the author's summary of the official reported court decision. However, a few case summaries have been acquired through conversations with attorneys or others involved in the actual litigation or from the sources cited. The reader is advised to consult the complete official court decisions for more details concerning each case.

The information presented in this handbook reflects the research and views of the author and is an attempt to simplify complex issues and concepts in order to assist criminal justice practitioners and agencies in developing a more proactive position relative to civil liability litigation. The information presented is for general information for training and educational purposes only and is *not* meant to be a source of legal advice of any kind. Each individual criminal justice practitioner or agency must consult an attorney for specific legal advice.

Contents

Introduction   *iii*

Chapter 1
Civil Liability Generally — 1
Crime versus Tort   1
Categories of Torts   2

Chapter 2
Civil Liability in Criminal Justice — 5
Negligence as a State Tort   6
Intentional State Torts   6
The Trend Today   7
42 United States Code, Section 1983   7
History of Section 1983   8
Current Status of Section 1983   9

Chapter 3
The Resuscitation of Section 1983 — 11
The Expansion of Section 1983   12
Other Developments   17
Impact   17

Chapter 4
Civil Rights Attorney's Fees Award Act of 1976   19
    The "American Rule"   21
    Impact of Section 1988   22
    Attorney's Fees for the Defendant?   23
    A Change in the Trend?   23

Chapter 5
Section 1983 Cause of Action   25
    Who Can Sue?   25
    Who Can Be Sued?   26
    Under "Color of State Law"   27
    The Doctrine of Respondeat Superior   28
    Personal Involvement Required   29
    The Magnitude of Section 1983 Litigation   30

Chapter 6
Section 1983 Actions in Corrections   33
    Physical Abuse   33
    Overcrowded Prisons   36
    Visitation and Use of the Mails   36
    Medical Care   37
    Cruel and Unusual Punishment   37
    Management Issues   38

Chapter 7
Section 1983 Actions in Law Enforcement   39
    Illegal Search and Seizure   39
    False Arrest   41
    False Testimony   42
    Police Brutality   42
    Wrongful Death Actions   44
    Off-Duty Activities   45

Chapter 8
Other Section 1983 Actions in Criminal Justice   49
    Judges   49
    Prosecutors   51
    Parole Officials   52
    Witnesses   53
    Legislators   53

CONTENTS *vii*

Chapter 9
The Emergence of Negligence as a Cause of Action Under Section 1983 — 55
- Degrees of Negligence and Extent of Damages   55
- Areas in which Negligence Leads to Liability   57

Chapter 10
Personal Liability of Administrators and Supervisors — 65
- Payment of Attorney's Fees   67
- Elements of a Personal Liability Lawsuit   67

Chapter 11
Personnel Issues Under Section 1983 — 71
- Non-Hire   72
- Non-Promotion   72
- Failure to Warn of Hazardous Work Conditions   72
- Discipline/Firing   73
- Due Process Requirements   76
- Exhaustion of Administrative Remedies   76

Chapter 12
Defenses and Lawsuit Prevention Strategies — 79
- Qualified Immunity   79
- The "Good Faith" Test   81
- An "Acceptable Beginning"   81
- Valid Authority   81
- Invalid Defenses   82
- Lawsuit Prevention   83
- Specific Proactive Principles   85
- Summary   87

Chapter 13
Trends — 89
- The Demise of the Exclusionary Rule   89
- Uncertainty and Continued Change in Section 1983 Applicability   90
- Lawyers Becoming More Knowledgeable About Section 1983   90
- Population Migration and Changes in Values   90
- The Growing Weight of Precedent   91
- Abuses Continue   91
- Failed Attempts to Set Liability Limits   92
- Other Developments   93
- Direction of the Trends   94

Chapter 14
Conclusion 97

References 99

Index 105

1 Civil Liability Generally

Law is divided into two parts: criminal law and civil law. Law enforcement officers and other criminal justice practitioners generally are more familiar with the criminal law because they deal with it daily. Civil law, however, may not be as familiar. It may be helpful, therefore, to compare criminal procedure with civil procedure.

Crime versus Tort

A crime is a *public* injury—an offense against the state—punishable by fine and/or imprisonment. It is a violation of the duty one owes the entire community; the remedy for a breach of such duty is punishment (fine or imprisonment), and such punishment can be administered only by the state.

A tort is a *private* injury—a wrongful act that results in injury or harm to the person or property of another. The injured party may sue in a *civil* action in order to recover damages from the offending party. The injured party initiates the lawsuit and is called the *plaintiff.* The person sued is called the *defendant* and is often referred to as the *tortfeasor.* The plaintiff sues for damages in an effort to be compensated for the harm caused by the defendant.

Originally, all crimes were torts. An injured party sought his own remedy, and the result often was feuding and fighting, which cost much in lives and property. Gradually the custom of private vengeance was replaced with the concept of criminal law—that is, the community as a whole is injured when one of its members is injured. Thus, the right to act against a wrongdoer was granted to the state as the representative of the people.

This concept did not replace the right of private redress. Therefore, a single act may be both a crime and a tort. For example, if X, in an unprovoked attack, injures Y, the state will attempt to punish X in a criminal action by sending him to prison, or fining him, or both. The burden of proof is for the state to establish the elements of the crime *beyond a reasonable doubt.* At the same time, Y, the victim, may sue X for money damages in a civil action for the personal injury he suffered. The basis of the complaint is that X failed to carry out his duty to Y to act reasonably and prudently and this failure resulted in Y's injury. This legal wrong is called a *tort.* Y must prove his claim by a *preponderance of the evidence.*

The major differences between criminal actions and tort actions are as follows:

- A criminal case is initiated by the state; it is always brought in the name of the state, the people, or the commonwealth. A tort case is initiated by the person who was injured and is brought in the name of that person.

- The remedy sought in a criminal case is the punishment of the wrongdoer in the form of a fine and/or imprisonment. The remedy sought by the plaintiff in a tort case is an award of money damages to be paid by the defendant.

- In a criminal case, the burden of proof on the state is proof *beyond a reasonable doubt.* In a tort case, the burden of proof on the plaintiff is a *preponderance of the evidence.*

- In a criminal case, the defendant may appeal a verdict against him, but the state has almost no right to appeal. In a tort case, *either* party may appeal.

Categories of Torts

There are, generally, three categories of torts that cover most of the suits against criminal justice practitioners. These three categories are *negligence, intentional torts,* and *constitutional torts.*

Negligence

Our society imposes a duty upon individuals to conduct their affairs in a manner that will avoid subjecting others to an unreasonable risk of harm. This also applies to criminal justice practitioners. If a law enforcement officer's conduct creates a danger recognizable as such by a reasonable officer in like circumstances, the officer will be held accountable to persons injured as a result of his conduct. In these situations, liability results because the officer failed to exercise due care and thereby created an unreasonable risk for others.

The degree of negligence can range from simple to gross and is determined on a case-by-case basis. *Simple* negligence means that the officer failed to exercise the due care that a *reasonable* officer would have exercised in similar circumstances, and an injury resulted. *Gross* negligence means that the officer acted recklessly, disregarding the consequences of his actions. In some cases, a tort that is the result of gross negligence is sometimes difficult to distinguish from an intentional tort because the disregard for the consequences often appears to be an intentional act. Criminal justice personnel are often sued for torts arising from negligent operation of motor vehicles, negligent training, negligent supervision, negligent failure to protect, and other such activities.

Intentional Torts

In negligence suits a defendant will not be liable unless he foresaw, or should have anticipated, that his act or omission would result in injury to another. An intentional tort, however, is the voluntary doing of an act which, to a substantial certainty, will injure another. It does not have to be done negligently to be actionable. Examples of such torts in the criminal justice area are assault and battery, false arrest, false imprisonment, malicious prosecution, abuse of process, wrongful death, and invasion of privacy.

Constitutional Torts

The duty to recognize and uphold the constitutional rights, privileges and immunities of others is imposed on law enforcement officers and other criminal justice practitioners by statute, and violations of these guarantees may subject the officers to civil suit. Most of these suits today are brought in federal court under Title 42 United States Code, Section 1983.

2 Civil Liability in Criminal Justice

Criminal justice practitioners have never enjoyed more than *qualified immunity* from civil liability litigation. Given the nature of their jobs, law enforcement officers and jail personnel are, and always have been, targets of such litigation. In the past, however, most civil suits were filed in state courts, with the plaintiff bringing a state tort action.

Such tort actions can be brought as a result of assault, battery, wrongful death, intentional infliction of emotional distress, failure to provide safety or medical care, or for failure to protect. Given the nature of law enforcement work, it is easy to see that law enforcement officers, jail personnel, and other criminal justice practitioners often engage in conduct within the scope of their duties that could (and does) lead to liability litigation. However, given the complex nature of state tort laws, which are often the result of an accumulation of years of court decisions, state courts have generally been kind to criminal justice practitioners and have required a high level of proof of wrongdoing in order for the plaintiff to prevail. Likewise, damages have generally been moderate.

In order for a plaintiff to prevail, he must show:

1. that the defendant owed him a *duty;*

2. that the defendant breached that duty;

3. that the breach of duty directly *caused harm* to the plaintiff, whether done purposely or done through negligence;

4. that the breach was the *proximate* (direct or legal) *cause* of the harm done; and

5. the plaintiff must prove the extent of the *damages* to be paid by the defendant.

Negligence and intentional torts are generally the only kind of state torts that are of concern to criminal justice practitioners, although there are other forms of torts under most state laws.

Negligence as a State Tort

Generally speaking, negligence under state law usually means that there is a breach of a statutory or common law duty to act reasonably toward those who may be harmed by a criminal justice practitioner. Therefore, even though the harm may be unintentional, liability can attach if it can be shown that the criminal justice practitioner's conduct created an unreasonable risk for others because of a lack of due care under the circumstances.

Negligence as a state tort action often results from the use or misuse of firearms, operation of motor vehicles in high-speed pursuits or in other dangerous or negligent ways, failure to provide adequate medical care, failure to respond to calls for assistance, or negligent failure to protect.

Intentional State Torts

An intentional tort is the voluntary doing of an act that, to a substantial certainty, will injure another. Unlike negligence, the mental state or "intent" of the criminal justice practitioner is important.

Liability suits of this nature often result from charges of excessive use of force, false arrest, false imprisonment, assault and battery, and wrongful death.

State tort law varies greatly from jurisdiction to jurisdiction, and the state courts are divided over issues dealing with whether a duty was owed to the individual plaintiff by the criminal justice practitioner, with the degree of negligence required in order for liability to attach, and with regard to the limits imposed on the amount of damages awarded. Even though the incidence of liability cases is on the rise, most suits against criminal justice personnel are unsuccessful.

The Trend Today

In the fairly recent past, the trend has been toward suing criminal justice personnel in federal court for alleged violations of constitutionally protected civil rights. In some ways it can be said that these suits are easier to win because the elements required for a successful cause of action appear to be easier to frame.

There are several federal statutes that allow citizens to bring actions against criminal justice practitioners in federal court. In some cases, the circumstances might warrant criminal charges against law enforcement personnel or other criminal justice practitioners, and there are criminal provisions in the federal statutes. However, the more common lawsuits filed in the federal courts against criminal justice personnel (and often their employing agencies as well) are civil suits and are generally referred to today simply as "Section 1983" actions.

Title 42 United States Code, Section 1983

The Statutory Language

> *Every person who, under color of any statute, ordinance, regulation, custom, or usage of any State or Territory, subjects, or causes to be subjected, any citizen of the United States or any other person within the jurisdiction thereof to the deprivation of any rights, privileges, or immunities secured by the Constitution and laws, shall be liable to the party injured in an action at law, suit in equity, or other proper proceeding for redress....*

The provision quoted above has been the basis of literally tens of thousands of lawsuits against criminal justice practitioners. Enacted in 1871, it was rarely used until the 1960s. Continued reinterpretation, renewed awareness of and concern for individual rights, and current legal doctrines and practices have made Title 42 United States Code, Section 1983 the most utilized and lucrative form of liability litigation against law enforcement officers, jail personnel, and other criminal justice practitioners.

History of Section 1983

In the years following the Civil War, Congress greatly broadened the scope of federal judicial authority. Among the legislation providing new sources of judicial power were several civil rights acts. The Act of 1871— embodying the current 42 U.S.C. Section 1983—provided a broad civil rights jurisdiction for all claims of deprivations of federally secured rights "under color of" state law.

Actually, the Act of 1871 was the Congressional reaction to the activities of the Ku Klux Klan and the inaction and powerlessness of the states to control such activities. The Ku Klux Klan Act of 1871 was enacted pursuant to the Fourteenth Amendment to provide a direct avenue to the federal courts for relief of alleged civil rights violations and reflected the Congressional hostility for, and distrust of, state courts. Although the Act was the subject of heated debate in Congress, Section I—today codified as 42 U.S.C. Section 1983—was the least controversial portion of the bill, as it only added civil remedies to the criminal penalties established by the 1866 Civil Rights Act.

The Act of 1871 was passed by Congress to provide civil rights protection against inaction and the toleration of private lawlessness. While the Act was intended to remedy the deficiencies of the southern states, there is little indication that Congress sought in any way to impair the states' political independence.

In fact, soon after the Civil War, the Supreme Court signaled its intention to return to the states the primary role in the area of civil rights and liberties through narrow readings of the Fourteenth Amendment (*Slaughterhouse Cases,* 83 U.S. (16 Wall.) 36 (1873), for example). The Court developed a doctrine that the Fourteenth Amendment could reach the conduct only of state governments and state officials and not private persons. Executive and judicial conduct sanctioned by the state was deemed to be "state action," but conduct by state officers in violation of their authority was not. In effect, the very lawlessness that was the primary target of the Act of 1871 was primarily immunized from federal sanction.

Through the period between the end of Reconstruction and the Depression, the federal judiciary seemed disposed to allow a wide latitude to state police power and placed a higher priority on maintaining a tranquil federalism than on the safeguarding of individual rights. Actions reminiscent of those perpetrated by the Klan were held to be beyond the scope of Section 1983. For example, *Brawner v. Irvin,* 169 F. 964 (1909), a Georgia case in which a Section 1983 action against a police officer who whipped and assaulted the female plaintiff in public, detained her, and eventually released her without charge was dismissed; the court saw no deprivation of any constitutionally or federally secured privilege or immunity.

This narrow construction of acting "under color of state law" received a major reinterpretation in 1941. In *United States v. Classic,* 313 U.S. 299 (1941), the Supreme Court reversed the dismissal of charges brought under the criminal provisions of the Civil Rights Acts against election officials who had fraudulently counted ballots in a primary—a clear violation of state law. The Court rejected the premise that "under color" of law required that the conduct be authorized by a state statute, stating that, "[m]isuse of power, possessed by virtue of state law and made possible only because the wrongdoer is clothed with the authority of the state, is action taken `under color of' state law" (313 U.S. at 326).

Four years later in *Screws v. United States,* 325 U.S. 91 (1945), the Court held that a sheriff's fatal beating of a black prisoner constituted conduct "under color" of the law. In effect, the Court, through Justice Douglas, defined "under color" of the law as meaning "under the pretense" of law.

Thus, at least in criminal actions under the Civil Rights Acts, conduct "under color of law" encompassed unauthorized, and indeed unlawful, conduct of a state officer, as long as the "pretense" of authority with which he acted furthered the constitutional violation in any way.

Decisions like *Classic* and *Screws* seemed to make Section 1983 increasingly more available for suits alleging police misconduct. In addition, in the years following the *Screws* decision, the gradual incorporation of the Bill of Rights into the due process clause, and the emergence of the modern equal protection and due process doctrines, greatly enlarged the potential reach of Section 1983. Still, Section 1983 was virtually ignored, and few cases seemingly were filed under it.

Current Status of Section 1983

Originally passed by Congress in 1871, and after being virtually ignored for nearly a century, Section 1983 has become second only to *habeas corpus* in the number of cases filed in the United States federal courts. The case that resuscitated the statute was *Monroe v. Pape* in 1961. This "resuscitation" came about during an era of heightened awareness of, and concern for, individual civil rights. The United States Supreme Court has continued to expand the scope of Section 1983 as the cases continue. Thus, it is an area of law undergoing a great deal of change and development. It is likely that cases like these will continue to increase in number and dollar amount. However, proper action could be taken by all criminal justice agencies that would virtually prevent all such suits from being filed; the criminal justice system (and the taxpayers who support it) would be much better off as a result.

3 The Resuscitation of Section 1983

After ninety years of relative inactivity, Section 1983 was resuscitated by the United States Supreme Court in 1961, and the seed for future fruition was sown.

Monroe v. Pape
365 U.S. 167 (1961)

In *Monroe v. Pape*, the plaintiff and his family sued 13 Chicago police officers and the City of Chicago, alleging that the law enforcement officers had broken into their home without a warrant, forced them out of bed at gunpoint, made them stand naked while the officers ransacked the house, and subjected the family to verbal and physical abuse. The police then allegedly took Monroe to the police station, where he was held incommunicado and interrogated for 10 hours before being released without being charged. Plaintiffs claimed that the defendants' actions constituted a deprivation, "under color of law," of their constitutional guarantee against unreasonable searches. The Federal District Court dismissed the complaint and the Court of Appeals affirmed. The United States Supreme Court heard the case and concluded that the law enforcement officers' conduct violated the plaintiff's constitutional rights. The Court held that the definition of "under color of law" for Section 1983 purposes was the same as that already established in the criminal context, and also concluded that because Section 1983 provides for a civil action, the plaintiffs need not prove that the defendants acted with a "specific intent to deprive a person of a federal right" (365 U.S. at 187). The Court also held, however, that municipalities (in this case, the city of Chicago) were immune from liability under the statute.

For 16 years following the Monroe decision, the federal courts, including the U.S. Supreme Court, continued to grant absolute municipal immunity. Thus, although it was clear that law enforcement officers and other criminal justice practitioners were subject to Section 1983 suits, it was also clear that a plaintiff usually would not be able to obtain sizable damages simply because criminal justice practitioners do not earn a great deal of money.

The Expansion of Section 1983

The portion of *Monroe* that granted municipalities and other local units of government immunity from Section 1983 actions was to be overruled in 1978, and the application of Section 1983 was to be greatly expanded. With the development of modern doctrines of "due process" and "equal protection" in an era of heightened awareness of individual liberties, the rapid and continued re-interpretation of Section 1983 by the United States Supreme Court has been observed since the late 1970s. Plaintiffs and their attorneys have also found the relative ease of framing a traditional state tort action into a constitutional claim and, thus, a Section 1983 cause of action.

Monell v. Department of Social Services
436 U.S. 658 (1978)

In *Monell* the petitioners, a class of female employees of the Department of Social Services and the Board of Education of the City of New York, commenced action under 42 U.S.C. Section 1983 in July 1971. The gravamen of their complaint was that the Board and the Department had, as a matter of official policy, compelled pregnant employees to take unpaid leaves of absence before such leaves were required for medical reasons. The suit sought injunctive relief and back pay for periods of unlawful forced leave. Named as defendants in the action were the Department and its Commissioner, the Board and its Chancellor, and the city of New York and its Mayor. In each case, the individual defendants were sued solely in their official capacities.

Although at first blush a case brought by a group of pregnant schoolteachers does not appear to have much to do with criminal justice practitioners, the decision of the Supreme Court was to have a tremendous effect. During the 16-year period that followed the *Monroe* decision, the federal courts, including the United States Supreme Court, had continued to grant absolute municipal immunity. However, in this case the Supreme Court overruled its previous decisions, stating:

> Our analysis of the legislative history of the Civil Rights Act of 1871 compels the conclusion that Congress *did* intend municipalities and other local government units to be included among those persons to whom Section 1983 applies. Local governing bodies, therefore, can be sued directly under Section 1983 for monetary, declaratory, or injunctive relief where, as here, the action that is alleged to be unconstitutional implements or executes a policy statement, ordinance, regulation, or decision officially adopted and promulgated by that body's officers. Moreover, although the touchstone of the Section 1983 action against a government body is an allegation that official policy is responsible for a deprivation of rights protected by the Constitution, local governments, like every other Section 1983 "person," by the very terms of the statute, may be sued for constitutional deprivations visited pursuant to governmental "custom" even though such a custom has not received formal approval through . . . official decision-making channels . . . . (436 U.S. at 690).

The Court went on to say:

> On the other hand, the language of Section 1983 read against the background of the same legislative history, compels the conclusion that Congress did not intend municipalities to be held liable unless action pursuant to official municipal policy of some nature caused a constitutional tort. In particular, we conclude that a municipality cannot be held liable solely because it employs a tortfeasor—or, in other words, a municipality cannot be held liable under Section 1983 on a *respondeat superior* theory (436 U.S. at 690-691).

Importance of the Monell *Decision*

Monell made it clear that a cause of action exists under Section 1983 where:

1. plaintiff has been deprived of a right, privilege or immunity secured by the Constitution and laws, and

2. such deprivation resulted from the official policy or custom of a local unit of government.

As a result of this ruling, Section 1983 plaintiffs now had a deeper pocket into which they could reach (i.e., the treasury of the local government unit), and with the earlier passage of the Civil Rights Attorney's Fees Awards Act of 1976 (Title 42 U.S.C. Section 1988, to be discussed later), suing law enforcement officers, jail personnel, and other criminal justice practitioners became more lucrative.

Owen v. City of Independence
455 U.S. 622 (1980)

Monell overruled *Monroe v. Pape* insofar as *Monroe* held that local governments were not among the "persons" to whom 42 U.S.C. Section 1983 applies and were therefore wholly immune from suit under the statute. *Monell* reserved decision, however, on the question whether local governments, although not entitled to absolute immunity, should be afforded some form of official immunity in Section 1983 suits. This action, *Owen v. City of Independence,* originally was brought in the District Court for the Western District of Missouri. On appeal, the Court of Appeals for the Eighth Circuit held that respondent, the city of Independence, Missouri, "is entitled to qualified immunity from liability" based on the good faith of its officials: "We extend the limited immunity the district court applied to the individual defendants to cover the City as well, because its officials acted in good faith and without malice." 589 F.2d 335, 337-338 (8th Cir. 1978).

The events giving rise to this suit were that the police chief of Independence, Missouri, and the new city manager engaged in a dispute about the manner in which the chief administered the police department's property room. A handgun, which the records of the department's property room stated had been destroyed, turned up in Kansas City in the possession of a felon. This discovery prompted the city manager to initiate an investigation of the management of the property room. Although the city auditor found that the police department's records were insufficient to permit an adequate accounting of the goods contained in the property room, the city counselor concluded that there was no evidence of any criminal act or of any violation of state or municipal law in the administration of the property room. Nevertheless, the city manager asked the chief to resign and to accept another position within the department, and warned that if the chief refused to take another position in the department his employment would be terminated, to which the chief responded that he did not intend to resign. The chief, having consulted with counsel, sent a letter to the city manager demanding written notice of charges against him and a public hearing with a reasonable opportunity to respond to those charges. However, at about the same time, the city council voted to release the investigative reports to the news media and to the prosecutor for presentation to the grand jury, and ordered the city manager to take "appropriate" action against those persons involved in illegal, wrongful, or grossly inefficient activities brought out in the investigative reports.

The city manager discharged the chief the next day. The chief was not given any reason for his dismissal; he received only a written notice stating that his employment as chief of police was terminated under the provisions of the city charter.

The local press gave prominent coverage to both the city council's action and the chief's dismissal, linking the discharge to the investigation. As instructed by the city council, the city manager referred the investigation to the prosecuting attorney of Jackson County, Missouri, for consideration by a grand jury. The results of the audit and investigation were never released to the public, however. The grand jury subsequently returned a "no true bill," and no further action was taken by either the city council or the city manager.

The petitioner named the city of Independence, city manager Alberg, and the present members of the city council in their official capacities as defendants in this suit. Alleging that he was discharged without notice of reasons and without a hearing, in violation of his constitutional rights to procedural and substantive due process, the petitioner sought declaratory and injunctive relief, including a hearing on his discharge, back pay from the date of discharge, and attorney's fees.

The case went to the U.S. Supreme Court, which reversed the Court of Appeals and held that the municipal corporation could not assert a "good faith" defense on the grounds that:

1. No such immunity existed at common law;

2. Congress desired wronged persons to be compensated;

3. Local governmental immunity would render Section 1983 an ineffective deterrent to violations; and

4. The principle of "equitable loss-spreading" requires no recognition of the immunity.

This holding was reached by the Supreme Court despite the absence of a finding that the violation was the "official policy" of the city, and despite its retroactive application of a new basis for liability (the requirement of a hearing prior to firing).

Maine v. Thiboutot
448 U.S. 1 (1980)

This case dealt with the phrase "and laws" in Section 1983. It had been assumed by most observers that the phrase meant laws pertaining to Constitutional rights.

The case presented two related questions arising under 42 U.S.C. Sections 1983 and 1988. Plaintiffs brought this suit in the Maine Superior Court, alleging that the state of Maine and its Commissioner of Human Resources violated Section 1983 by depriving plaintiffs of welfare benefits to which they were entitled under the federal Social Security Act. The case presented two issues: (1) whether Section 1983 encompassed claims based on purely statutory violations of federal law, and (2) if so, whether attorney's fees under Section 1988 may be awarded to the prevailing party in such an action. The Supreme Court held:

> The question before us is whether the phrase "and laws," as used in Section 1983 means what it says, or whether it should be limited to some subset of laws. Given that Congress attached no modifiers to the phrase, the plain language of the statute undoubtedly embraces [plaintiffs'] claim . . . . Even were the language ambiguous, however, any doubt as to its meaning has been resolved by our several cases suggesting, explicitly or implicitly, that the Section 1983 remedy broadly encompasses violations of federal statutory as well as constitutional law . . . (100 S. Ct. at 2504).

The Court went on to rule that as the "prevailing party," the plaintiffs were entitled to an award of attorney's fees.

The impact of *Monell, Owen* and *Thiboutot* is that a Section 1983 action against a unit of government alleging a deprivation of rights granted by the Constitution or any federal statute may be brought and the defendant government unit may not assert a "good faith" defense, even if the action was not unconstitutional when it occurred. And, if the plaintiff prevails, the government must also pay his attorney's fees.

Other Developments

There have been further developments in this area of the law. In 1981 municipalities were held to be immune from punitive damages in a Section 1983 suit in *City of Newport v. Fact Concerts, Inc.* 101 S. Ct. 2748 (1981). Also in 1981, a United States District Court ruled that a plaintiff need not establish a Section 1983 claim, but may sue a local unit of government directly under a *respondeat superior* theory in *Rhodes v. City of Wichita* 516 F. Supp. 501 (D. Kan. 1981). In addition, the Third Circuit held that a state has *parens patriae* standing to bring Section 1983 suits against local governmental officials' violations and misconduct in *Pennsylvania v. Porter* 659 F.2d 306 (3d Cir. 1981), *cert. denied,* 102 S. Ct. 3509 (1982). In 1986, the Supreme Court stated that the "official policy" requirement of *Monell* was intended to distinguish acts of the *municipality* from the acts of the municipality's *employees (Pembaur v. City of Cincinnati,* 475 U.S. 469, 1986). In *City of Canton v. Harris* 489 U.S. 378 (1989), the Court held that the "inadequacy of police training may serve as the basis for Section 1983 liability only where the failure to train in a relevant respect amounts to deliberate indifference to the constitutional rights of persons with whom the police come into contact." 489 U.S. at 388-389. The emergence of negligence as a cause of action has also contributed to the development of this area of the law.

Impact

The number of these cases continues to increase for several reasons. Under the rubric of "due process," or "equal protection," almost any common law tort committed by a state or local government official can be converted into a constitutional violation, and thereby made the basis of a Section 1983 action. Also, money damages are usually sought (especially if the "deep pocket" of the local government unit can be tapped)—that is, *somebody* will have to pay if the plaintiff wins. By being able to proceed directly in federal court, more liberal rules of discovery are made available and overburdened state courts (and their generally more conservative rules and judges) are avoided. An appearance of widespread abuse arises and plaintiffs can be given a sense of unity and moral support if the case is filed as a *class action,* which is a lawsuit brought by or on behalf of a group of similarly situated plaintiffs. Finally, if the plaintiff prevails, he or she will be entitled to receive attorney's fees in addition to the relief given or the damages received. This encourages attorneys to take on suits that show promise of success.

All of these factors place a great deal of stress on an individual or agency named in a suit. The individual practitioner who has few personal resources or insurance can be extremely vulnerable to this stress—especially if he or she has little support from the employing agency.

Many times an agency (or local unit of government) will settle out of court in order to avoid adverse publicity or to avoid the expense and stress of going to trial. Actually, only a very small percentage of the civil rights cases that are filed ever get to trial. For example, according to the Federal Judicial Center (1980), only 3.5 percent of cases initiated by state prisoners went to trial in 1979, and, although the *number* of cases appears to be on the rise, the *percentage* actually going to trial has apparently not increased greatly. Nevertheless, much stress results and often large sums of money are spent in preparing and defending such suits, and often the terms of a settlement are not revealed.

4 Civil Rights Attorney's Fee Award Act of 1976

Passage of Title 42 United States Code, Section 1988 (the Civil Rights Attorney's Fees Awards Act of 1976) and the broad application of it by federal courts have encouraged even more litigation, resulting in awards of extremely high attorney's fees. The pertinent part of the Act provides:

> ... In any action or proceeding to enforce a provision of sections 1981, 1982, 1983, 1985 and 1986 of this title ... the court, in its discretion may allow the prevailing party, other than the United States, a reasonable attorney's fee as part of the costs.

Congress enacted this statute in 1976 to "encourage private attorneys general to enforce fundamental constitutional rights under Section 1983," *Riddell v. National Democratic Party*, 624 F. 2d 539, 543 (5th Cir. 1980), and to encourage "compliance with and enforcement of the civil rights laws," *Dennis v. Chang*, 611 F.2d 1302 (9th Cir. 1980). The courts have struggled at times to determine what factors should be considered in setting "reasonable" fees under the act.

Johnson v. Georgia Highway Express
488 F.2d 714 (1974)

This Fifth Circuit case has often been cited in attorney's fees cases. Even though the case predated passage of Section 1988 it dealt with a very similar statute, Section 706(k) of Title VII of the Civil Rights Act of 1964 (42 U.S.C. § 2000e-5(k)). This statute reads:

> In any action or proceeding under this subchapter the court, in its discretion, may allow the prevailing party . . . a reasonable attorney's fee as part of the cost of the litigation . . .

Although it has been somewhat modified in recent years, the case presented a series of factors that the Fifth Circuit felt should be considered in awarding attorney's fees, including:

1. **The time and labor required.** Although hours claimed or spent on a case should not be the sole basis for determining a fee, they are an ingredient to be considered. The trial judge should weigh the hours claimed against his own knowledge, experience, and expertise of the time required to complete similar activities.

2. **The novelty and difficulty of the questions.** Cases of first impression generally require more time and effort on the attorney's part. Although this greater expenditure of time in research and preparation is an investment by counsel in obtaining knowledge that can be used in similar later cases, he or she should not be penalized for undertaking a case that may make new law.

3. **The skill required to perform the legal service properly.** The trial judge should closely observe the attorney's work product, his preparation, and general ability before the court.

4. **The preclusion of other employment by the attorney due to acceptance of the case.** This guideline involves the consideration of otherwise available business which is foreclosed because of conflicts of interest that occur from the representation, and the fact that once the employment is undertaken the attorney is not free to use the time spent on the client's behalf for other purposes.

5. **The customary fee.** The customary fee for similar work in the community should be considered.

6. **Whether the fee is fixed or contingent.** The fee quoted to the client or the percentage of the recovery agreed to is helpful in demonstrating the attorney's fee expectations when he accepted the case.

7. **The amount involved and the results obtained.**

8. **The experience, reputation, and ability of the attorneys.** Most fee scales reflect an experience differential with the more experienced attorneys receiving larger compensation. An attorney specializing in civil rights cases may enjoy a higher rate than others due to his expertise, providing his ability corresponds with his experience.

9. **The "undesirability" of the case.** A civil rights attorney faces hardships in his community because of his desire to help the civil rights litigants, and often his decision to help eradicate discrimination is not favorably received by the community or his contemporaries. This can have an economic impact on his practice that can be considered by the Court.

10. **Awards in similar cases.** The reasonableness of a fee may also be considered in light of awards made in similar litigation in that circuit and other circuits.

The "American Rule"

Not all courts view the awarding of attorney's fees in the same light. The United States Supreme Court case that follows was the primary ruling that motivated Congress to enact 42 U.S.C. Section 1988

Alyeska Pipeline Service Co. v. Wilderness Society
421 U.S. 240 (1975)

This litigation was initiated by Wilderness Society, Environmental Defense Fund, Inc., and Friends of the Earth in an attempt to prevent the issuance of permits by the Secretary of the Interior that were required for the construction of the trans-Alaska oil pipeline. The Court of Appeals awarded attorneys' fees to respondents against petitioner Alyeska Pipeline Service Co. based upon the court's equitable powers and the theory that respondents were entitled to fees because they were performing the services of a "private attorney general." The United States Supreme Court reversed the decision, stating that the "American Rule" was that the prevailing litigant ordinarily is *not* entitled to collect attorneys' fees from the loser. That is to say, each side pays its own attorneys' fees. The Court went on to state:

> Although . . . Congress has made specific provision for attorneys' fees under certain federal statutes, it has not changed the general statutory rule that allowances for counsel fees are limited to the sums specified by the costs statute . . . (421 U.S. at 254-255).

Thus, according to the Court, Congress has fully recognized and accepted the general rule, but has made specific and explicit provisions for the allowance of attorneys' fees under selected statutes granting or protecting various federal rights. The Court also determined that the circumstances under which attorneys' fees are to be awarded and the range of discretion of the courts in making those awards are matters for Congress alone to determine, stating that ". . . the 'American Rule' . . . followed in our courts with respect to attorneys' fees has survived. It is deeply rooted in our history and in congressional policy; and it is not for us to invade the legislative's province by redistributing litigation costs . . ." (421 U.S. at 271).

In reaction to this case, Congress enacted 42 U.S.C. Section 1988. Thus, although the case seemed to shut the door on the awarding of fees, its impact had the opposite effect.

The Impact of Section 1988

However meritorious the original purpose of Section 1988, in practice, broad judicial application of it has led to questionable results. Courts have awarded bonuses, or multipliers, reflecting such factors as the unpopularity or complexity of the case when awarding attorney's fees under Section 1988. For example:

> In *Ruiz v. Estelle,* 553 F. Supp. 567 (S.D. Tex. 1982), the Federal District Court found that it was "reasonable" to enhance the award of fees by use of a multiplier of two, resulting in an award of attorney's fees in excess of $1.6 million

It must be noted, however, that even though $1.6 million appears to be an excessive fee, this particular case was in the courts for years, the state of Texas attempted to avoid payment in a variety of ways, including the passage of an act by the legislature to limit or deny payment, and the amount of money spent by the state in this action was much higher than this award. In short, the *apparent excess* may well have been appropriate. Therefore, many of the examples of excessive fees need to be reviewed carefully.

Courts have, however, also awarded attorneys' fees that greatly exceeded the amount of damages awarded to the plaintiff:

In *Coop v. City of South Bend*, 635 F.2d 652 (7th Cir. 1981) the court approved an award of $6,000 in attorney's fees although the plaintiff recovered only $510 in compensatory damages. In *Copeland v. Marshall*, 641 F.2d 880 (D.C. Cir. 1980), the plaintiffs recovered $33,000 in back pay and the approved attorney's fees were $160,000 Also, in *McNamara v. Moody*, 606 F.2d 621 (5th Cir. 1979) the court awarded $6,500 in attorney's fees when the plaintiff was awarded nominal damages of $1.

Courts also have allowed the awarding of attorney's fees where the plaintiff was represented by a publicly funded legal service organization (*David v. City of Scranton*, 638 F.2d 676, 3d Cir. 1980); where the suit resulted in a consent decree with no admission of fault (*Massachusetts Fair Share v. O'Keefe*, 476 F. Supp. 294, D. Mass. 1979); and where defendant's unilateral or legislative actions moot the case (*William v. Alioto*, 625 F.2d 845, 9th Cir. 1980, *cert. denied*, No. 80-653).

Attorney's Fees for the Defendant?

The phrase "prevailing party" in 42 U.S.C. Section 1988 has basically been interpreted by the courts to mean "the prevailing plaintiff." Essentially, the defendant in a Section 1983 case rarely will be awarded attorney's fees if he successfully defends the lawsuit. About the only way for a criminal justice practitioner defendant to be awarded attorney's fees is if he can prove the suit against him was totally without merit. That is, the defendant must prove to the satisfaction of the court that there was absolutely no merit to the plaintiff's case, that the plaintiff filed the suit only to harass the defendant, or that the suit was brought by the plaintiff for vindictive purposes. Generally, therefore, criminal justice practitioner defendants will almost never be awarded attorney's fees if they win their cases because the courts usually find that the matters alleged needed to be looked into, even if not proven.

A Change in the Trend?

The United States Supreme Court may well have signaled a change in the trend in the case of *Hensley v. Eckerhart*, 461 U.S. 423 (1983). The Court, perhaps concerned about the trend in awarding very high attorney's fees, made clear to the lower courts that the degree of success should be the key factor to consider when awarding attorney's fees. The Court stated:

> Where the plaintiff has failed to prevail on a claim that is distinct in all respects from his successful claims, the hours spent on the unsuccessful claim should be excluded in considering the amount of a reasonable fee . . . . [T]he district court should award only that amount of fees that is reasonable in relation to the results obtained . . . (461 U.S. at 440).

The Court did not rule out any of the other *Johnson* factors, but clearly stated that the degree of success (i.e., the results obtained) should be the most important factor to consider. *Blum v. Stenson,* 465 U.S. 886, 104 S. Ct. 1541 (1984) appeared to underscore the Court's intention to adhere to this line of thinking, but in *Venegas v. Mitchell* 495 U.S. 82 (1990), the Court said that Section 1988 does not invalidate a contingency fee contract that would require a prevailing plaintiff to pay his attorney more than the statutory award against the defendant. Therefore, the Court evidently decided that in passing Section 1988 Congress intended that a "reasonable fee" awarded under Section 1988 be merely a credit against larger contingency fees agreed to prior to trial.

Regarding the lodestar approach to determining reasonable attorney fees, lower courts have discussed acceptable factors for it. In *Davis v. Locke* 936 F.2d 1208 (11th Cir. 1991), the court rejected any comparison of the claims with the results obtained, saying that the deterrent effect might well be as important as the monetary damages recovered, and upheld a $62,000 fee award. In *Leffler v. Meer,* 936 F.2d 981 (7th Cir. 1991), the court decided that the relative simplicity of the case, the brevity of the trial, a contingency fee contract and the relationship between the fees sought and the relief obtained ($1.8 million vs. $33,000) all justified the reduction of the billable hours. In *Hendrickson v. Branstad,* 934 F.2d 158 (8th Cir. 1991), the court refused to limit the plaintiff's attorney's rate to the local market rate because he was determined to be a national expert in this area of the law and, therefore, entitled to be paid at a rate usually charged by nationally prominent attorneys. However, the court did refuse to apply a requested 25 percent multiplier because the record did not reflect evidence of exceptional results.

5 Section 1983 Cause of Action

Section 1983 does "not provide for any substantive rights—equal or otherwise" *Chapman v. Houston Welfare Rights Organization,* 441 U.S. 600 at 617 (1979). Rather, it is a remedial device that affords the party seeking relief for the deprivation of a constitutional (or federal statutory) right a mechanism through which to obtain such relief. What elements must be shown to establish a cause of action under Section 1983? The elements are essentially as follows:

1. The plaintiff must be a "person protected" by the act.
2. The defendant must be a "person" within the meaning of the act.
3. The defendant must have been "acting under color of law" when the alleged deprivation took place.
4. The alleged deprivation must be a deprivation of "any rights, privileges, or immunities secured by the Constitution and laws."
5. The plaintiff may seek money damages, injunctive relief, or "other proper proceeding for redress."

Who Can Sue?

Section 1983 authorizes relief to "any citizen of the United States or any other person within the jurisdiction thereof. . . ." Thus, it appears that anyone subject to the jurisdiction of the United States is a "person protected" by the act. That means that citizens, or anyone else living in this country (even illegal aliens) can sue under Section 1983. It would also appear that business and nonprofit corporations and even unions are "persons" who may sue under Section 1983, given the fact that corporate "persons" are recognized in other areas of American law.

Although there currently is great pressure to redefine the status of an unborn fetus, the Supreme Court held in *Roe v. Wade* 410 U.S. 113 (1973), that "the word 'person' as used in the Fourteenth Amendment, does not include the unborn" 410 U.S. at 158. As a result, it would appear that an unborn fetus is not a "citizen" or "other person" within the meaning of the act and no suit therefore, could be brought on behalf of an unborn child.

An interesting situation has developed in the Third Circuit, where it has been decided that the state can bring a Section 1983 action under a *parens patriae* theory. The Third Circuit Court of Appeals held that a state may sue when it seeks to advance "significant sovereign interests of its own in the prevention of further violation of constitutional rights of its citizens," if it cannot reasonably anticipate that normal law enforcement will protect those interests. *Pennsylvania v. Porter,* 659 F.2d 306, 316 (3d Cir. 1981) (*en banc*), *cert. denied,* 102 S. Ct. 3509 (1982). Few, if any, cases have attempted to proceed on the *Porter* theory, but if cases do prevail under *Porter,* the state, through a civil rights or public advocate's division of an Attorney General's office, *could* ring Section 1983 suits to vindicate widespread constitutional violations (e.g. widespread abuses by municipal police or local jail personnel).

Who Can Be Sued?

The statute clearly states that "every person" (acting under color of state law) who causes another to be deprived of a federal constitutional or statutory right is liable and, therefore, can be sued under Section 1983. Inasmuch as virtually every criminal justice practitioner acts "under color of" state law, each individual criminal justice practitioner is liable under the statute, including all law enforcement officers, jail personnel, sheriffs, police chiefs, supervisory personnel, and state officials in criminal justice agencies (e.g., Commissioner of Corrections).

The law recognizes corporate "persons" as well as natural persons and, at least since *Monell,* it is clear that such corporate persons are liable under the provisions of Section 1983. This means that municipalities, counties, and other units of local government may now be sued for injunctive, declaratory, and monetary relief. It has also been held that suits against government officials in their official capacities are tantamount to suits against the unit of government. *Universal Amusement Co. v. Hofheinz,* 646 F.2d 996 (5th Cir. 1981); *Will v. Michigan Department of State Police,* 491 U.S. 58 (1989).

However, the state itself is not subject to a Section 1983 suit. According to *Alabama v. Pugh,* 438 U.S. 781 (1978), the Eleventh Amendment bars a suit against a state under Section 1983. But while the Amendment prohibits suits in law or equity, it does not bar prospective equitable relief against state officials, even when compliance will require the expenditure of state funds. The state may, of course, waive its Eleventh Amendment immunity or it may be forced to do so under Section 5 of the Fourteenth Amendment, which gives Congress the power to enact legislation to carry out the Fourteenth Amendment. Because prospective relief is not barred and because 42 U.S.C. Section 1988 was enacted under Section 5, it has been held, for example, that the state of Arkansas would have to comply with the federal court's mandate to upgrade its prison system. The court stated, "If Arkansas is going to operate a penitentiary system, it is going to have to be a system that is countenanced by the Constitution of the United States." *Finney v. Arkansas,* 505 F.2d 194 at 199 (8th Cir. 1974). In *Hutto v. Finney,* 437 U.S. 687 (1978), the Supreme Court upheld this concept by ruling that a claim for attorney's fees under 42 U.S.C. Section 1988 is not barred by the Eleventh Amendment because it was enacted under Section 5 of the Fourteenth Amendment.

Any ambivalence with regard to this issue was settled by the Supreme Court in *Will v. Michigan Department of State Police,* 491 U.S. 58 (1989) when the Court stated, ". . . a State is not a person within the meaning of Section 1983. 491 U.S. at 64. The Court also stated that, obviously, ". . . state officials literally are persons. But a suit against a state official in his or her official capacity is not a suit against the official but rather against the official's office. . . . As such, it is no different from a suit against the State itself." 491 U.S. at 71.

Under "Color of State Law"

The lawsuit must allege that the act committed by the defendant was "under color of" state law. Early cases ruled that executive and judicial conduct sanctioned by the state was a "state action," but conduct by state officers in violation of their authority was not. In effect, the very lawlessness of government agents, the primary target of the Act of 1871, was effectively immunized from federal sanction.

"Misuse of power, possessed by virtue of state law and made possible only because the wrongdoer is clothed with the authority of state law, is action taken 'under color of' state law," *United States v. Classic*, 313 U.S. 299 at 326, 61 S. Ct. 1031 at 1043 (1941). This statement was quoted in *Monroe v. Pape* as the correct meaning of "under color of" in Section 1983. Thus, any misuse or abuse of power is now deemed to be action taken "under color of" state law. Private citizens cannot be sued under Section 1983 for nonstate-related activities unless they conspire with state officers. See *Slavin v. Curry*, 574 F.2d 1256 (5th Cir., 1978).

Section 1983 does not apply to federal officials, because they generally act under color of federal law and the act requires that the person act under color of state or territorial (or District of Columbia) law. As a general matter, state and local officials acting in their official capacities are persons who act under color of state law, and private persons who act in concert with state officials act under color of law as well. Thus, virtually all actions performed by criminal justice practitioners will be construed to be action taken under color of state law, inasmuch as virtually all criminal justice activity is performed by public sector personnel rather than by private parties. Such actions are likely not only to bring about liability to the offending officer, but to his or her employing agency as well.

The Doctrine of Respondeat Superior

A defendant is not liable solely under the doctrine of *respondeat superior*. In *Monell*, the Supreme Court said "a municipality cannot be held liable *solely* because it employs a tortfeasor—or, in other words, a municipality cannot be held liable under Section 1983 on a *respondeat superior* theory" (435 U.S. at 691). Therefore, simply employing someone who engages in unconstitutional behavior is not sufficient to make a local unit of government liable. It is, rather, when execution of a government's policy or custom, whether made by its lawmakers or by those whose edicts or acts may fairly be said to represent official policy (such as police chiefs, sheriffs, mayors, council members, etc.), inflicts the injury, that the local unit of government is responsible under Section 1983.

However, the U.S. District Court for the District of Kansas has ruled that a plaintiff need not establish a Section 1983 claim, but may sue a local government directly under a *respondeat superior* theory. *Rhodes v. City of Wichita*, 516 F. Supp. 501 (1981). At this point, *Rhodes* seems to be a one-of-a-kind decision and has not prevailed outside the Kansas District.

Rizzo v. Goode
423 U.S. 362 (1976)

The Supreme Court held in *Rizzo v. Goode* that the mere right to control, without any control or direction having been exercised and without any failure to supervise, is not enough to support Section 1983 liability under the doctrine of *respondeat superior.*

"Persons" other than municipalities are not liable for money damages under the doctrine of *respondeat superior.*

Personal Involvement Required

Generally, personal involvement by the defendant is required in order for the plaintiff to bring a successful Section 1983 suit. The following cases illustrate this point.

Williams v. Anderson
599 F.2d 923 (10th Cir. 1979)

In this case the prison timekeeper made a mistake that resulted in a prisoner being held beyond the expiration of his sentence. Where there was nothing to indicate that reliance on the timekeeper was unreasonable, the other prison officials could not be held vicariously liable for the mistake.

Taken Alive v. Litzau
551 F.2d 196 (8th Cir. 1977)

The plaintiff in *Taken Alive v. Litzau* claimed that she suffered injuries during the course of an arrest. Her Section 1983 lawsuit against the Chief of Police was for his alleged negligent supervision (i.e., his negligent failure to supervise, direct, control or limit the improper actions of Officer Litzau). The evidence showed that the Chief did not cause, encourage, initiate, consent to, authorize, direct, or command Officer Litzau or any other person to arrest the plaintiff by use of unreasonable force. In order to prevail on this aspect of her Section 1983 claim, the plaintiff had to prove actual involvement of the Chief in the alleged misconduct.

Ford v. Byrd
544 F.2d 194 (5th Cir. 1976)

A chief of police is liable for the acts of his subordinates (in this case, a search) only if he directs, orders, participates in, or approves the acts, according to *Ford v. Byrd.*

The *respondeat superior* theory has not been successfully utilized (with the exception of *Rhodes v. Wichita, supra*) in Section 1983 litigation. However, as will be presented later, if negligence in direction or supervision can be shown, the supervisor *can* be held liable for the acts of his or her subordinate. Negligence is the key factor, because the supervisor is liable for his or her act or failure to act when he or she knew or should have known of the subordinate's behavior or actions that resulted in the deprivation of another's rights. The relief granted can be money damages, injunctive or declaratory relief, or other proper redress.

The Magnitude of Section 1983 Litigation

The Number of Cases

After nearly a century of inactivity, the number of Section 1983 actions has increased dramatically since the *Monroe* decision, and especially since the decisions in *Monell, Owen,* and *Thiboutot.* A survey conducted by the International Association of Chiefs of Police showed that the number of civil liability suits against police increased from 1,741 in 1967 to over 3,800 in 1971. According to Kappeler (1993), there were over 13,400 civil suits filed against law enforcement officers in 1976, and Americans for Effective Law Enforcement (1980) predicted that in the 1980s there would be over 26,000 civil lawsuits filed against the police annually. Even those estimates appear to be conservative, as Silver (1991) reports that there are now more than 30,000 civil actions filed against the police annually. All of these studies concern *only the police* and do not include suits against correctional personnel, probation and parole officers, and others in the criminal justice system.

The Costs

A survey in 1981 by the National Institute of Municipal Law Officers (NIMLO) of its members, revealed that there were civil liability litigation claims in excess of $4.3 billion pending against only 215 municipalities. There are more than 39,000 local units of government in the United States, and if all are being sued at approximately the same rate, there could be as much as $780 billion in Section 1983 claims pending. Even assuming that only one percent of the amounts of claims ripen into judgment, some $7.8 billion in local tax-raised revenues could be spent in paying Section 1983 claims (Bates, 1981).

This speculative figure, of course, does not include the additional costs of:

1. the defendant's legal fees;

2. court-awarded attorney's fees under Section 1988;

3. other relief as the court deems just;

4. the amounts involved in suits directly against individuals (the amount reported in the NIMLO survey was only the amount of damage claims against local units of government).

In 1982 there were over 250 cases in which juries awarded $1 million or more (NCW, 1985), and del Carmen (1991) reported that an average jury award of liability against a municipality rose from $230,000 in 1982 to $2 million in 1985. Clearly, Section 1983 suits have the potential to bankrupt a municipality. If the municipality goes to court with the case, it must pay the costs involved in providing its defense. Should it lose the case, the plaintiff's attorney's fees, as well as the damages awarded, must also be paid. Even if the case is settled out of court, the municipality might well have to pay plaintiff's attorney's fees in addition to the amount of the settlement and the fees of its own attorneys. The settlement also provides a precedent, and it is not unusual to see a number of suits filed after a settlement in one suit has been reached. In any event, even if the municipality successfully defends the suit, the costs are great and can place a burden upon the resources available.

Many municipalities attempt to avoid large judgments by settling claims out of court for a small portion of what a jury might award. For example, the city of New Orleans agreed to pay $2.8 million to settle 13 cases alleging police brutality (*Crime Control Digest,* April 14, 1986). Obviously, with an average jury award of $2 million, the potential for 13 awards could have been at least $26 million and the city settled for only 10 percent of that figure. While this practice may appear to save money, it can also lead to paying large sums of money even in cases in which a jury might well have found that there was no wrongdoing on the part of the criminal justice personnel sued. Even a settlement is considered a "win" by the plaintiff, and as Lynn Lund (1982) put it, "when you lose the first big cases, other claims fall around your head like rain." Even so, given the potential of multi-million dollar jury awards and the cost of the litigation itself, many municipalities choose not to gamble and continue to settle out of court while attempting to identify frivolous suits that arise as a result. The most unfortunate result of this activity is the loss of confidence from the general public that this engenders because a settlement is perceived by the public to be an admission of guilt. This also extracts a tremendous toll in the form of lower morale of criminal justice practitioners who feel abandoned by their employing municipality. These are costs that cannot be measured in terms of dollars alone.

There is absolutely nothing in the trends to indicate that civil liability suits against criminal justice practitioners, agencies, and their employing municipalities will begin to decrease. The costs will also continue to increase, both in monetary and non-monetary terms.

6 Section 1983 Actions in Corrections

Inmates in jails and correctional institutions can bring Section 1983 suits against prison or jail personnel and administrators for alleged deprivations or violations of rights secured under the Constitution or federal laws. Inadequate prison or jail conditions, such as poor plumbing, poor lighting, unsanitary conditions or food, and grossly overcrowded conditions can be deemed a Section 1983 violation of the Eighth Amendment prohibition against "cruel and unusual punishment." Thus, just as law enforcement officers find themselves potentially liable in many aspects of their everyday duties, jail and correctional personnel also are placed in such situations as a result of their duties and responsibilities. In fact, the early successful Section 1983 actions were filed by prison inmates, and cases continue to be filed from behind the prison walls.

Physical Abuse

Placing inmates in cells with other inmates who have known dangerous or violent propensities can be the basis for a Section 1983 lawsuit.

Smith v. Wade
103 S. Ct. 1625 (1983)

This was a case against a correctional officer for placing inmates with known dangerous propensities in a cell with the plaintiff. The jury found the defendant correctional officer (Smith) liable and awarded $25,000 in compensatory damages plus $5,000 in punitive damages. The United States Supreme Court affirmed the decision and held that a jury may be permitted to award punitive damages in an action under Section 1983 when the defendant's conduct is shown to be motivated by an evil motive or intent, or when it involves reckless or callous indifference to the federally protected rights of others. Likewise, overlooking continued abuse or sexual activity of prisoners can be the basis for such a suit. Needless to say, abuse by jail personnel renders each one liable, and if lack of training or negligence in supervision can be shown, liability can be passed up the chain of command.

Physical abuse by correctional personnel also is a basis for a Section 1983 suit.

Owens v. Haas
601 F.2d 1242 (1979)

In *Owens*, plaintiff Owens was a federal prisoner who was cooperating with the United States government. In order to insure his safety, he was transferred from federal prison to the Nassau County Jail in Hicksville, New York. Approximately two months after being sent to the Nassau County Jail, Owens was awakened by a corrections officer and told to report to the court desk to sign for a warrant that had been lodged against him. Owens refused to leave his cell, believing that he did not have to sign for a warrant. Sometime later, Correctional Officer Haas came to his cell, and when Owens again refused to leave, Haas told him to pack up his "stuff" because he was being moved. Insults were exchanged when Owens refused to leave and Officer Haas left.

Fifteen to twenty minutes later, several officers returned to Owens' cell and ordered him to leave. An argument ensued, and Owens stepped out of his cell. Approximately seven correctional officers were present. Owens was grabbed and beaten severely by the officers, resulting in lacerations, bruises, and lasting impairments that caused him to suffer blackouts.

The court ruled that the County of Nassau should be held liable if the failure to supervise or the lack of a proper training program was so severe as to reach the level of "gross negligence" or "deliberate indifference" to the deprivation of the plaintiff's constitutional rights. The court went on to say that a "causal link" must be made between the county's failure to train and the violation of constitutional rights, and a single brutal incident such as this "may be sufficient" to suggest that link. The failure to train or supervise law enforcement officers must be so grossly negligent as to constitute "deliberate indifference" in order to hold the county liable, but the court felt that the circumstances of this severe beating were such as to suggest "official acquiescence" on some level. Owens was permitted to conduct a limited discovery to determine if such a case could be made.

In *Benny v. Pipes,* 799 F.2d 489 (9th Cir. 1986), *cert. denied,* 108 S. Ct. 198 (1987) it was alleged that a correctional officer's failure to intervene and stop the assault of a prisoner by another prisoner, and a "minor" assault by a correctional officer, represented a violation of substantive due process or the Eighth Amendment. When no answer was filed by the officers, Benny obtained a default judgment of $2,000. Because it was a default judgment, the Ninth Circuit took the allegations to be true. Thus, according to the court, Benny stated a substantive due process claim as well as an Eighth Amendment claim (*Police Misconduct and Civil Rights Law Report,* Vol. 2, No. 6, at 62, November-December, 1987).

Force used by a correctional officer against a prisoner need not cause "significant injury" to be cruel and unusual punishment under the Eighth Amendment, and if the force is applied "maliciously and sadistically" for the purpose of causing harm, it can result in a Section 1983 action.

Hudson v. McMillian
503 U.S. 1 (1992)

In *Hudson v. McMillian,* a prisoner in Louisiana brought a Section 1983 action for excessive use of force, alleging that correctional officer McMillian punched him in the mouth, eyes, chest, and stomach while another officer held him. This beating split Hudson's lower lip, loosened his teeth, and cracked his partial dental plate. The second correctional officer kicked Hudson in the rear, while a supervisor looked on and joked with the other officers.

A magistrate heard the case and accepted Hudson's testimony over that of the officers and found that the officers used forced when there was no need for it and that the resulting injuries were minor. A judgment of $800 in damages was awarded. On appeal, the Fifth Circuit reversed, stating that although the court "joins the magistrate in deploring the use of unnecessary force in the treatment of prisoners . . . not every use of excessive force rises to a constitutional violation cognizable under 42 U.S.C. Sec. 1983." 929 F.2d at 1015. The court then reversed the magistrate's decision.

The United States Supreme Court, on February 25, 1992, reversed the Court of Appeals and stated that when prison officials "maliciously and sadistically use force to cause harm, contemporary standards of decency always are violated . . . This is true whether or not significant injury is evident" (Slip Opinion at 6). Lack of "significant injury" was improperly used, said the Court, to dismiss the prisoner's claim.

Overcrowded Prisons

Placing an inmate in an overcrowded facility is also a proper basis upon which to file a Section 1983 lawsuit, and can escalate into a complex and expensive settlement. In *Nelson v. Leeke, Commissioner, South Carolina Department of Corrections* (U.S. Dist. Ct., S.C. District, Number 82-876- 2), the settlement enumerated 238 identifiable issues in 17 categories and was estimated to cost the state over $78 million to comply. The first quarterly compliance report totaled 141 pages and required an untold number of man-hours to compile (Office of the Executive Assistant to the Commissioner for Legal Settlements and Compliance, 1985).

Visitation and Use of the Mails

It is clearly established law that unless the jail or prison administrators can clearly show that the security or proper discipline of the institution is threatened, it is a violation of constitutional rights to deprive an inmate visitation privileges or the use of the mails or telephone.

McNamara v. Moody
606 F.2d 621 (5th Cir. 1979)

McNamara, a prisoner in the Glades Correctional Institution at Belle Glade, Florida, brought suit against two officials of that institution, charging that they had wrongfully prevented him from mailing certain letters. Moody, the assistant superintendent of Glades, refused to mail a letter to McNamara's girlfriend. This two-page letter dealt in large part with McNamara's discontent with the prison mail censorship system, but it also charged that the mail censoring officer, while reading mail, engaged in masturbation and "had sex" with a cat. Moody found the part of the letter referring to the officer to be "in poor taste" and returned it to McNamara with a warning that future attempts to send similar letters would lead to disciplinary action.

The court stated that the law in this area is "well settled" and that prison censorship of prisoner mail is strictly limited. It (1) must further an important or substantial governmental interest unrelated to the suppression of expression; and (2) the limitation of First Amendment freedoms must be no greater than is necessary or essential to the protection of the particular governmental interest involved. Moody's argument that to allow letters such as this one would result in a "total breakdown in prison security and discipline" was rejected, as was his contention that the letter was libelous and obscene. The court stated that letters could not be suppressed simply because they were defamatory, and although the letter was vulgar, it was not obscene. Therefore, it was ruled that Moody had not established a "substantial" government interest in suppressing McNamara's letter.

McNamara was awarded nominal damages of $1. However, being the "prevailing party" in the action, he was also awarded $6,500 in attorney's fees. The awards were assessed against Moody in both his official capacity and in his individual capacity, the court stating that he had acted in "objective bad faith" and therefore was personally liable.

Medical Care

Failure to provide adequate medical care has also been utilized as a basis for liability litigation. It may not be necessary to have a physician on duty in the jail, but it is clear that there must be access to a physician or a paramedic. In addition, jail personnel must be properly trained to recognize medical problems.

Dewell v. Lawson
489 F.2d 877 (10th Cir. 1974)

In *Dewell*, the court held that an alleged failure to establish procedures and to train personnel to protect prisoners from medical injuries due to inattention established a cause of action under Section 1983. The plaintiff was a diabetic who went into a coma and was permanently paralyzed as a result of alleged inattention on the part of city jail personnel.

In this case, the supervisor was held liable for failure to train and supervise his subordinates. It would appear that the standard of liability for failure to properly train is less than that required to show "cruel and unusual punishment."

Cruel and Unusual Punishment

The Eighth Amendment prohibition against "cruel and unusual" punishment has been utilized often as a cause of action under Section 1983.

1. Overcrowding. Grossly overcrowded conditions can be an example of a violation of Section 1983 under the Eighth Amendment (see *Nelson v. Leeke, supra*). Also, incidents

arising from overcrowded conditions—such as assaults, increased homosexuality, increased violence within the facility—can be a Section 1983 violation of the Eighth Amendment.

2. Inadequate jail conditions, such as poor plumbing, lighting, food, and medical care, can be made into Eighth Amendment violations.

   a. A Section 1983 action can prevail for one inadequate jail condition if it is gross or clearly outrageous—that is, a condition that would shock the conscience of a reasonable and prudent man.

   b. Additionally, a "totality" of several less severe conditions can add up to an unconstitutional jail.

On June 18, 1993, the United States Supreme Court ruled in *Helling v. McKinney,* No. 91-1958, 53 CrL 2230, that prisoners can use the Eighth Amendment's ban on cruel and unusual punishment as a basis for suing their custodians over the adverse long-term health effects that allegedly result from involuntary exposure to secondhand tobacco smoke. The prisoner need not show that the condition he challenges has caused a current health problem; conditions that pose serious threats to his future health are also actionable under Section 1983. The prisoner in this case complained of being celled with a five-pack-a-day smoker and claimed "deliberate indifference" on the part of prison officials. The Court stated, "[w]e have great difficulty agreeing that prison authorities may not be deliberately indifferent to an inmate's current health problems but may ignore a condition of confinement that is sure or very likely to cause serious illness and needless suffering the next week or month or year" (53 CrL 2232).

Management Issues

Virtually every aspect of the management of a jail or prison facility can be a potential Section 1983 action. However, in *Bell v. Wolfish,* 441 U.S. 520 (1979), the Supreme Court ruled that a "rational basis" and not a "compelling governmental necessity" is the proper test to determine whether regulations and practices amount to punishment. Also, *Hudson v. Palmer,* 468 U.S. 517 (1984), and *Block v. Rutherford,* 468 U.S. 576 (1984) seem to indicate a continuing trend to allow correctional administrators to operate their facilities without frequent intervention from the federal courts.

7 Section 1983 Actions in Law Enforcement

There is no group of workers, public or private, that is more susceptible to liability litigation than law enforcement officers. Because of the nature of their duties, it is no coincidence that law enforcement officers find themselves defendants in civil suits. Given the complex nature of the unenviable tasks they must perform, it is simply impossible for law enforcement officers to flawlessly perform their duties; mistakes are inevitable.

Of course, there are overzealous officers, and officers who ignore the rights of those with whom they deal. Given the hit-or-miss recruitment of law enforcement officers and the uneven level of training afforded from one department to another, it is not surprising that outrageous police conduct comes before the courts more often than honest, "good faith" mistakes.

Recent liability suits against law enforcement officers have focused on six areas of police misconduct: illegal search and seizure, false arrest, false testimony, police brutality, wrongful death actions, and off-duty activities. All of these unfortunate actions are potential consequences arising out of a law enforcement officer's official responsibilities.

Illegal Search and Seizure

Search and seizure is one of the more complicated issues with which a law enforcement officer must deal. The standards that apply in search and seizure cases seem to vary greatly, depending upon the facts of each case. All cases require a showing of probable cause, but what exactly constitutes probable cause? The general rule requires the issuance of a warrant, but there are "exigent circumstances" that allow for searches and seizures without the issuance of a warrant. Who knows precisely what "exigent circumstances" are?

Judges, lawyers, and scholars have debated these questions time and again with no precise, all-inclusive answers forthcoming. Nevertheless, law enforcement officers are subject to Section 1983 litigation if they engage in what a court later determines to be an illegal search or seizure. *Monroe v. Pape* and other cases clearly establish this.

Section 1983 actions are becoming more numerous in alleged illegal search and seizure cases. Unlike the exclusionary rule, Section 1983 actions (and damages) are available to innocent persons subjected to illegal searches and seizures as well as to guilty persons. In addition, given the recent erosion of the exclusionary rule, it can be expected that Section 1983 cases will continue to increase in this area in an effort to deter police misconduct. Again, unlike exclusionary rule cases, Section 1983 suits hit the offending law enforcement officer directly in his or her pocketbook, and usually provide the victim with the "deep pocket" of the employing agency.

Duncan v. Barnes
592 F.2d 1336 (5th Cir. 1979)

In this case, police officers obtained a warrant to search a suspect's premises for heroin. The apartment was described as an upstairs apartment when in fact the suspect lived in a downstairs apartment. The Plainview, Texas, officers executed the warrant in the early morning hours. With a sledge hammer, they broke down the rear door of an apartment belonging to three students. With guns drawn, the officers proceeded to break down the doors to two bedrooms in the apartment, forcing the occupants, two females and one male, to stand nude, spread-eagled against a wall while the rooms were searched. After several minutes, the police were satisfied that they had entered the wrong apartment and left. The apartment was in disarray: the doors were smashed, the television and tape recorder were broken, and other personal property was damaged. The students were so upset that they were forced to miss the next two weeks of classes.

The police argued that they had "acted in good faith" with a "reasonable" belief that the warrant was valid; therefore, no liability should attach to their actions. The court stated that even if it were true that the warrant was valid, the officers could be liable under Section 1983 if the valid warrant "is executed in an unreasonable manner."

False Arrest

The general rule seems to be that a law enforcement officer is not liable under Section 1983 simply because he arrests someone, unless the officer violated clearly established law. Discretionary acts, including the decision to arrest, are cloaked with a qualified "good faith" immunity from civil liability. *Saldana v. Garza,* 684 F.2d 1159 (5th Cir. 1982), *cert. denied,* 460 U.S. 1012 (1983). However, when the acts are negligent, unresponsive to legitimate requests, or indifferent to a person's rights, a different picture emerges.

Murray v. City of Chicago
634 F.2d 365 (7th Cir. 1980)

In this case, the plaintiff's purse and checkbook were stolen, and the theft was reported to the police. Six to twelve months later, some of the stolen checks were cashed at various retail stores, and the plaintiff was arrested. All but one charge was dismissed, but thinking that all the charges had been dismissed, plaintiff did not appear at the next hearing and a warrant was issued for her arrest. Learning of this development, plaintiff appeared in court and the warrant was quashed and the remaining charge against her was dismissed.

Several months later, the plaintiff was arrested at her home by two Chicago police officers, pursuant to the invalid warrant. Plaintiff was taken to headquarters, forced to strip naked and submit to searches conducted and observed by male police officers. She was imprisoned for six to seven hours before being released.

The court ruled that the police officers were acting in good faith, but that if the policy, custom, or practice of the city could be established to show that other unwarranted arrests have occurred frequently, the city could be held liable.

Powe v. City of Chicago
664 F.2d 639 (7th Cir. 1981)

Powe was the victim of an armed robbery. The robber took Powe's wallet and identification. When later arrested for another charge, the robber used Powe's identification, entered a plea of guilty, and was sentenced to two years probation under Powe's name. He then violated the conditions of probation and an arrest warrant was issued.

Powe was stopped for a traffic violation sometime later, and when the police officer learned that there was an outstanding warrant for him, placed him under arrest. Powe was able to substantiate his story and was released. However, he was arrested three months later under similar circumstances. The court ruled that the municipality must be held liable under Section 1983 if the factfinder determines that its procedures led to the issuance of an invalid warrant, and thereby, to unlawful arrests. Given the allegations contained in Powe's complaint, the court stated that such a conclusion would be permissible.

Even if the person arrested enters a guilty plea to the charge, he or she is not barred from bringing a Section 1983 claim against the law enforcement officer who made a false arrest according to the Supreme Court. (*Haring v. Prosise,* 103 S. Ct. 2368 (1983).

False Testimony

Law enforcement officers enjoy absolute, unqualified immunity from Section 1983 liability for giving false testimony. In *Imbler v. Pachtman,* 424 U.S. 409, 96 S. Ct. 984 (1976) and *Briscoe v. LaHue,* 103 S. Ct. 1108 (1983), the United States Supreme Court ruled that law enforcement witnesses, like all other witnesses, must be free from liability. The logic is simple: the rigors of cross-examination and the penalties for perjury provide substantial checks against false testimony by witnesses.

Police Brutality

Section 1983 has been clearly recognized as the appropriate avenue for redressing police brutality, because these activities are exactly the kind of deprivations of "rights, privileges, or immunities" that the law was designed to prevent. The following cases reported by Lloyd (1983) illustrate the types of brutality cases and the damages that have been awarded.

Gilliam v. Falbo (U.S. District Court, S.D. Ohio, April, 1982, filed in 1977, was a Section 1983 action in which a young man, beaten with blackjacks by two police officers suffered a concussion and lacerations. After years of offering to settle the case for $3,000, on the day of the trial the defendants offered to settle for $72,500 which the plaintiff accepted.

In *Motley v. McCallum* (Wayne County, Michigan, No. 79-719-897-NO, January, 1982), the plaintiff was arrested for DUI and, while at the police station, he had a fistfight with an officer who hit him in the head with a blackjack. The plaintiff suffered brain damage. Plaintiff's evidence showed that there had been negligent use of excessive force; also that the department provided no training or policy guidelines either for dealing with intoxicated persons or for use of blackjacks. Furthermore, there had been no departmental investigation or disciplinary action with respect to the incident. SETTLEMENT: $1,205,000.

Saddlewhite v. City of Los Angeles (1982), was a Section 1983 action in which an adult male was beaten by the police and suffered facial cuts and bruises. SETTLEMENT: $30,000.

In *Herbert v. City of Texas City,* U.S. District Court, S.D. Texas, 1981, a police officer broke the arm of the man he was arresting. Suit was filed, alleging brutality on the part of the arresting officer. JURY AWARD: $151,000

A Section 1983 action was filed by a 35-year-old black plaintiff who, after being subjected by police to racial slurs and epithets, was beaten and chained to a bed for twelve hours without criminal charges being filed. The plaintiff suffered a fractured jaw and psychiatric illness (traumatic neurosis). *Haygood v. City of Detroit,* Wayne County Circuit Court, Michigan, No. 77-728013 NO, December 29, 1980. JURY AWARD: $2,500,000 punitive and $500,000 compensatory damages.

In *Parsons v. Pfeiffer* (U.S. District Court, N.D. Illinois, 1975), the defendant police officer found a car blocking his automobile's path in a service station. He pulled the plaintiff out of the car and beat him over the head with a four- pound radio. The plaintiff suffered a "spastic neck," resulting in his having to carry his head at an angle. He claimed $600 in lost income for his two-week recovery, and $1,500 in medical bills. JURY AWARD: $100,000.

Jennings v. City of Detroit, Wayne County Circuit Court, Michigan, August, 1979, was a Section 1983 action in which a 22-year-old black man was permanently paralyzed after being beaten at a police station. JURY AWARD: $8,000,000; settled for $3,500,000.

In *Jones v. City of Santa Monica* (Santa Monica Superior Court), a jury awarded $209,883 against the city for a police officer's use of a flashlight to strike a truck driver who allegedly used obscene gestures toward the officer. The truck driver was not in any way involved in the accident the officer was investigating, but the injuries allegedly resulting from the officer's attack included brain damage, seizures, broken facial bones, and $98,000 in medical bills (*Liability Reporter,* Number 229, January, 1992, p. 3).

Zimmerman (1990) reports compensatory damage awards in the following nonfatal use of force cases.

In *Gutierrez-Rodriguez v. Cartagena,* 882 F.2d 553 (1st Cir. 1989), $4.5 million was awarded to a shooting victim who was rendered paraplegic; *Languirand v. Hayden,* 717 F.2d 220 (5th Cir. 1983), a $1.5 million verdict in a police shooting (reversed on other grounds); *Davis v. Little,*

851 F.2d 605 (2d Cir. 1988), in which a police officer shot a fleeing suspect and shattered his elbow, resulting in an award of $347,000; *Hall v. Ochs,* 817 F.2d 920 (1st Cir. 1987), awards of $160,000 in compensatory and $200,000 punitive damages for false arrest and $50,000 in compensatory and $10,000 in punitive damages for beating with racial motivation; and in *Herrera v. Valentine,* 653 F.2d 1220 (8th Cir. 1981), in which $300,000 was awarded to a pregnant woman who was kicked in the stomach and abdomen and thrown to the ground, resulting in a miscarriage.

Wrongful Death Actions

Clearly, if use of excessive force or "brutality" is a proper cause of action under Section 1983 then wrongful death actions are as well. Lloyd (1983) reports the following cases involving wrongful death actions.

Prior v. Woods (U.S. District Court, E.D. Michigan, 1981), was a Section 1983 action in which a white, 24-year-old man was shot to death outside his home in July, 1979, by police officers who mistook him for a burglar. JURY AWARD: $5,750,000.

In *Crockett v. Dade County,* Dade County Circuit Court, Florida, 1976, a youth was apparently stealing a car when the police intervened. An officer in the path of the car fired five shots at the driver and his two companions. The boy died later of a severed spinal cord, and his parents filed suit. JURY AWARD: $300,000.

In *Ryer v. Sweeny,* Los Angeles County Superior Court, California, June, 1973, police officers raided the apartment directly above that of the deceased's mother-in-law. While lowering his AR-15 rifle to the floor, one officer accidentally discharged a bullet that passed through the floor, grazing the head of a 22-month-old infant and killing the father in the apartment below. JURY AWARD: $900,000.

In *Barrales v. Morris,* United States District Court (N.D. Illinois, 1979), the police went to a suspect's hotel room to question him about a rape. The man fled to the bathroom. When the police entered the bathroom, the man fell or was pushed from the window to his death. The police said that he either jumped or fell, but the jury evidently believed that he was pushed and awarded $1,500,000.

In *Burkholder v. City of Los Angeles,* 1982, a Los Angeles police officer shot and killed a white man in his early twenties who, while naked and under the influence of PCP, was climbing a lamp post; the man had seized the officer's billy club, but had not struck the officer. Victim's mother and daughter brought the action, and the jury awarded $450,000 in damages and $150,000 in attorney's fees.

Zimmerman (1990) reports that in *Roman v. City of Richmond*, 570 F. Supp. 1544 (N.D. Cal. 1983) an award of $3 million was awarded in the police killing of two black men. Other cases and the compensatory damage awards reported by Zimmerman (1990) include *Graddstaff v. City of Borger*, 767 F.2d 161 (5th Cir. 1985), *cert. denied*, 480 U.S. 916 (1987) in which $1.43 million was awarded for the shooting of an innocent person during a chase; *Bell v. City of Milwaukee*, 746 F.2d 1205 (7th Cir. 1984), a 20-year cover-up of the use of a drop knife following a police shooting which determined that damages were not limited by the state wrongful death act and awarded $100,000 to the estate of the victim, $540,000 to the siblings for the conspiracy, and $300,000 to the victim's father's estate; and *Urseth v. City of Dayton*, 680 F. Supp. 1150 (S.D. Ohio 1987) in which $1.65 million was awarded for shooting and cover-up.

In *Swann v. City of Goldsboro*, U.S. District Court (E.D.N.C., No. 90-59-CIV-5-D, April 2, 1991), the city settled for $220,000 on a claim that the police officers' lack of training in CPR resulted in the arrestee's death (*Liability Reporter*, Number 229, January, 1992, p. 7).

High-speed chases also often result in injuries and deaths, and liability can result. A Wayne County Circuit Court jury awarded $1.95 million to the family of a woman killed in a high-speed chase involving police from Detroit and suburban Dearborn Heights (*Crime Control Digest*, January 6, 1992, p. 9). In *Moses v. City of Chicago*, police officers engaged in a 70 mile-per-hour chase of a car that failed to dim its lights and then fled. During the chase, the officers ducked below the dashboard after hearing what they believed to be shots from the car being chased (no evidence of any shots being fired could be found). The officers entered an intersection and went through a red light at 70 miles per hour—still below the dashboard, and collided with a vehicle occupied by a seven- year-old and his parents. Both mother and father were killed, and the child has had 39 operations, suffers from learning and social disabilities, and has accumulated medical bills of $181,000 and is expected to have medical bills of $55,000 per year for the foreseeable future. The city settled for $3.65 million (*Liability Reporter*, Number 239, November, 1992, p. 167).

Off-Duty Activities

Even when off-duty, law enforcement officers can be held liable under Section 1983 if their conduct is deemed to be under color of law. Thus, working part-time as a security officer, making an arrest or intervening in a situation while off duty, or accidentally causing an injury with a service revolver have all been held to be acting under color of law. In many cases, the police chief or sheriff, as well as the employing local unit of government, has also been held liable.

Hacker v. City of New York
261 N.Y.S.2d 751 (1965)

A police officer's wife was injured when the officer's service revolver discharged as he was cleaning it at home. This was ruled "within the scope of his duties" and the city was liable.

Carmelo v. Miller
569 S.W.2d 365 (Mo. 1978)

Two off-duty officers were working as security officers at a baseball game. The officers received information that someone was displaying a gun at one of the concession stands. The information included the description of the two men, a Mexican wearing a red shirt and black pants and a black male wearing gold-colored pants. After the game in a nearby parking lot, the plaintiff (a Mexican wearing a red shirt and black pants) and his black companion, wearing gold pants, were stopped, searched, and arrested even though neither had a gun and none was found in the area. Plaintiff claimed he was beaten and kicked and sustained injuries requiring medical treatment. The police officers were held liable for damages under Section 1983.

Stengle v. Belcher
522 F.2d 438 (6th Cir. 1975)

An off-duty police officer entered a bar with his girlfriend and was seated with another couple in one of the booths. The officer was out of uniform but was equipped with a can of mace and a .32 caliber revolver, that police regulations required him to carry at all times. An altercation broke out in the bar. Without identifying himself as a police officer at any time, the officer involved himself in the altercation. When the dust settled, the officer had killed two men and seriously wounded another. Plaintiffs recovered $800,000 in compensatory damages and $3,000 in punitive damages.

Many police departments require their employees to be "on-duty" twenty- four fours a day by requiring them to make arrests or intervene in any unlawful situations they observe whether during their "on-duty" shift or not. Also, most off-duty employment is gained by reason of having a uniform and apparent authority, and agency-issued equipment is often used in these off-duty employment settings. Therefore, the courts rarely have difficulty in finding that an off-duty officer acts under color of law. If the officer is in violation of departmental regulations, however, he may find that he is alone with regard to liability for actions taken while off duty. For example, if departmental policy does not allow off-duty employment or does not allow the use of uniforms, weapons, or other equipment issued by the department to be used in off-duty employment and an officer utilizes it anyway, the department may be dismissed from the suit.

In *Domashewsky v. Sierociuk,* Cook County Circuit Court, No. 84L-24504, March 26, 1991, the village was found liable for $850,000 for the shooting of an intoxicated man by an off-duty auxiliary police officer acting as a hotel security officer (*Liability Reporter,* Number 229, January, 1992, p. 8). However, in *Sawyer v. Humphries* (Maryland Court of Appeals, No. 44-1990, March 22, 1991), the Maryland court ruled that the principle that a Maryland state police officer is "on duty" at all times does not mean that everything he does is within the scope of his employment so as to make him immune from suit under the state's tort claims act. In this case, an off-duty officer threw rocks at the plaintiff's car and attacked him and his passenger. The court stated that the officer was "acting for personal motives" and in no way was furthering the state's interest (49 CrL 1017).

8 Other Section 1983 Actions in Criminal Justice

Some criminal justice officials, like judges, prosecutors, and parole officials, enjoy absolute immunity from liability. The decisive factor is the function performed by the official, not his or her title. (See *Supreme Court of Virginia v. Consumers Union,* 446 U.S. 719 (1980); *Butz v. Economou,* 438 U.S. 478 (1978)).

Judges

Judges are absolutely immune from liability for their judicial acts under Section 1983 as long as they do not act in clear absence of all jurisdiction.

Pierson v. Ray
386 U.S. 547 (1967)

In *Pierson v. Ray,* several black ministers on a "prayer pilgrimage" from New Orleans to Detroit were arrested in Jackson, Mississippi, for disobeying a sign at the entrance of the bus terminal that announced "White Waiting Room Only—By Order of the Police Department," and attempting to enter the terminal restaurant and refusing to "move on" as ordered by two police officers. The ministers were tried by a "municipal police justice" who found them guilty of breach of the peace. On appeal and trial *de novo* the County Court reversed the convictions and a Section 1983 action was instituted against the arresting officers and the judge. The U.S. Supreme Court had no difficulty in finding that the judge was immune from liability for damages for his role in these convictions because all he did was adjudge them guilty when their cases came before him. Stating that judicial immunity from liability for damages for acts committed within their judicial jurisdiction is a doctrine solidly established at common law, the Court added that a judge's errors may be corrected on appeal, but a judge should not have to fear that the unsatisfied litigants might hound him with litigation, charging malice or corruption. The Court went on to say that it did not believe that this settled principle of law was abolished by Section 1983.

Stump v. Sparkman
435 U.S. 349 (1978)

In this case, a judge of a state court of general jurisdiction was deemed to be absolutely immune from liability for issuing an order of sterilization, despite the lack of statutory authority for the order. Whether the judge acted with malice was irrelevant, said the Court, because he did not act in clear absence of jurisdiction, but merely in excess of jurisdiction. Such action was not sufficient to deprive him of his immunity.

A judicial act is one usually performed by a judge. However, judges also perform functions that are not considered judicial acts. In cases involving nonjudicial acts, a judge has no immunity.

Zarcone v. Perry
581 F.2d 1039 (2d Cir. 1978)

In *Zarcone*, the judge dispatched a deputy sheriff to purchase coffee from a mobile food vending truck in front of the courthouse. Dissatisfied with the coffee, which the judge described as "putrid," he ordered the deputy sheriff and two other deputies to bring the vendor to his chambers through the crowded courthouse in handcuffs and then tongue-lashed the vendor, threatening him with legal action and the loss of his livelihood. An hour later the judge again summoned the vendor before him and sought an admission that something was wrong with the coffee. The vendor consistently refused to admit that anything was wrong with the coffee. As a result of this incident, the vendor alleged that he suffered from anxiety, persistent headaches and stuttering, required treatment in a hospital, experienced marital difficulties, and was unable to work. The jury awarded the vendor $80,000 in compensatory damages, $60,000 in punitive damages against the judge, and $1,000 in punitive damages against the deputy sheriff. (See also *Beard v. Udall,* 648 F.2d 1264 (9th Cir. 1981) in which a judge made a prior agreement to decide a case in a particular way.)

Likewise, judicial immunity is no bar to an award under Section 1988 for costs and attorneys' fees incurred in obtaining *injunctive* relief against a judge.

Pulliam v. Allen
466 U.S. 522 (1984)

In this case the plaintiffs, former county jail inmates, brought a Section 1983 action against a Virginia magistrate, claiming that her practice of imposing bail on persons arrested for non-jailable offenses and incarcerating them if they could not make bail, violated both equal protection and due process principles. Agreeing with the plaintiffs, the district court enjoined the practice and awarded attorney's fees of more than $7,000. The U.S. Court of Appeals for the Fourth Circuit affirmed, rejecting the magistrate's contention that judicial immunity precluded the award. The United States Supreme Court affirmed on May 15, 1984. Thus, judicial immunity is not a bar to prospective injunctive relief against a judicial officer acting in a judicial capacity, nor is it a bar to the award of attorneys' fees under 42 U.S.C. Section 1988. Judges are absolutely immune *only* from liability for money damages for any official judicial act they perform.

Prosecutors

Prosecutors are also absolutely immune for activities that are "intimately associated with the judicial phase of the criminal process." *Imbler v. Pachtman,* 424 U.S. 409, at 430 (1976). Included among these activities is the decision to prosecute as well as decisions made during the actual prosecution of the case. It would appear, however, that a prosecutor only enjoys *qualified* immunity for his administrative and investigative functions, because these acts are not "intimately associated" with the judicial function (e.g., investigative actions are generally treated the same as such activities by law enforcement officers, and administrative duties—"running the office"—are not absolutely immune from liability). See *Mancini v. Lester,* 630 F.2d 990 (3d Cir. 1980).

In *Burns v. Reed,* 111 S. Ct. 1934 (1991) the Supreme Court ruled that a state prosecuting attorney is absolutely immune from liability for damages under Section 1983 for participating in a probable cause hearing, but not for giving legal advice to the police. The Supreme Court seems to be uninterested in extending absolute immunity unless there are substantial justifications for doing so (111 S. Ct. at 1939). It would appear that prosecutorial liability will continue to be a case-by-case, fact-bound inquiry. So far, there is no definitive test for distinguishing between conduct closely related to the initiation of a prosecution, and actions that are investigative or given as legal advice to investigators. If the prosecutor engages in investigative actions, he will have the same degree of immunity as an investigator—qualified, good faith immunity.

Parole Officials

Parole officials likewise enjoy absolute immunity because they perform tasks comparable to judges when they decide to grant, deny, or revoke parole. *Sellars v. Procunier,* 641 F.2d 1295 (9th Cir.), *cert. denied,* 454 U.S. 1102 (1981).

Martinez v. California
444 U.S. 277 (1980)

This case arose out of the murder of a 15-year-old girl by a parolee. Her survivors brought a Section 1983 action claiming that the state officials responsible for the parole-release decision were liable in damages for the harm caused by the parolee.

The parolee, Thomas, was convicted of attempted rape, committed to a state hospital as a "mentally disordered sex offender not amenable to treatment" (444 U.S. at 279) and thereafter sentenced to a term of imprisonment of one to twenty years, with a recommendation that he not be paroled. Nevertheless, five years later, he was paroled to the care of his mother. The parole board was fully informed about his history, his propensities, and the likelihood that he would commit another violent crime. Five months after his release, Thomas tortured and killed the girl. Calling the parole board's action not only negligent, but reckless, willful, wanton, and malicious, the girl's survivors sued for actual and punitive damages of $2 million.

The Supreme Court stated that although the decision to release Thomas from prison was action by the State, ". . . the action of Thomas five months later cannot be fairly characterized as state action"(444 U.S. at 285). The

Court went on to say that, "... it is perfectly clear that not every injury in which a state official has played some part is actionable under [Section 1983]" (444 U.S. at 285).

A state parole officer, however, has only qualified immunity from a complaint alleging that he violated a parolee's constitutional rights by keeping him in custody pending a revocation proceeding before the parole board. Such conduct is not close enough to any quasi-judicial function to merit absolute immunity (*Mee v. Ortega,* 51 CrL 1353, 6/18/92).

Therefore, the actions of parole or probation officers that are not considered to be quasi-judicial in nature, but rather tend to be investigative or enforcement oriented, will result in the same degree of immunity enjoyed by law enforcement officers—a qualified, good faith immunity.

Witnesses

Witnesses generally have been entitled to absolute immunity, even if they commit perjury, because there are sufficient checks and balances and penalties available. Witnesses are expected to testify truthfully, and should not be placed under the additional pressure that they might be sued for so testifying. *Briscoe v. LaHue,* 103 S. Ct. 1108 (1983).

Legislators

Legislative officials enjoy absolute immunity for their legislative acts. *Supreme Court of Virginia v. Consumers Union, supra; Tenney v. Brandhove,* 341 U.S. 367 (1951).

9

The Emergence of Negligence as a Cause of Action Under Section 1983

Negligence has now emerged as a viable cause of action in Section 1983 litigation. Actually, *Monroe v. Pape* is the starting point, because the Supreme Court stated that Section 1983 "should be read against the background of tort liability that makes a man responsible for the natural consequences of his actions" 81 S. Ct. at 494. Further, the Court stated:

> It is abundantly clear that one reason the legislation [Section 1983 was passed was to afford a federal right in federal courts because by reason of prejudice, passion, neglect intolerance or otherwise, state laws might not be enforced and the claims of citizens to the enjoyment of rights, privileges, and immunities might be denied. . . . *Monroe v. Pape*, 365 U.S. 167 at 180, 81 S. Ct. 473 at 480 (1961) [Emphasis added].

Degrees of Negligence and Extent of Damages

There are various levels or degrees of negligence recognized in the law. Basically, these are "simple" negligence, "gross" negligence, and "willful" or "criminal" negligence. The chart that follows shows the levels of negligence, the types of damages that may ordinarily be recovered, and who generally pays the damages.

ACTION	DAMAGES	WHO PAYS
SIMPLE NEGLIGENCE		
A reasonable act by a reasonable officer in the scope of his or her employment, but without due care	Actual only: some states allow mental pain and anguish damages	Employer or insurance company
GROSS NEGLIGENCE		
An unreasonable act: must be clear as a matter of law	Actual, plus mental pain and anguish damages	Employer may or may not—depends on whether the conduct was within the scope of employment
WILLFUL NEGLIGENCE		
(Actually an intentional act rather than negligence) A gross act done intentionally	Actual, plus mental pain and aguish, plus punitive damages	Individual pays—Employer or insurance company cannot be made to pay (Exceptions rare)

Twenty years after *Monroe*, in *Parratt v. Taylor*, 451 U.S. 527 (1981), the Supreme Court stated that "[n]othing in the language of Section 1983 or its legislative history limits the statute solely to intentional deprivations of constitutional rights" (451 U.S. at 534).

The law now seems conclusive that not only can a person be liable under Section 1983 for negligent acts that result in the violation of someone else's rights, but also that a supervisor or administrator can be held liable for his own personal negligent conduct that was the proximate cause of a subordinate's actionable conduct. See *McClelland v. Facteau*, 610 F.2d 693 (10th Cir. 1979)] *Owens v. Haas*, 601 F.2d 1242 (2d Cir. 1979); and *Brandon v. Allen*, 16 F. Supp. 1355 (W.D. Tenn. 1981).

Areas in which Negligence Leads to Liability

There are numerous areas in which negligence can lead to a cause of action under Section 1983. The following list is not all-inclusive, but is merely representative of the types of negligence theories that are being successfully presented in the federal courts.

Negligent Hiring

The law enforcement or jail administrator and the local governmental agency have an affirmative duty to "weed out" those who are obviously unfit. *Peters v. Bellinger,* 159 N.E.2d 528 (Ill. App. 1959).

Negligent Assignment

If the supervisor knew or should have known, or if a subordinate is obviously unfit for an assignment, then there is an obligation to change that subordinate's assignment. *Moon v. Winfield,* 383 F. Supp. 31 (N.D. Ill. 1974).

Negligent Retention

If a subordinate is obviously unfit for service, then there is an obligation to terminate the employee. *Murray v. Murphy,* 441 F. Supp. 120 (E.D. Pa. 1977).

Negligent Entrustment

Administrators, supervisors, and government agencies have a duty to properly supervise errant off-duty officers where an officer has property— e.g., a gun, car, or nightstick—belonging to the governmental agency. *Allen v. City of Los Angeles,* No. C-9837 (L.A. Sup. Ct., 1975); *Stengel v. Belcher,* 522 F.2d 438 (6th Cir. 1975).

Negligent Direction

A written manual of policies and procedures is an absolute must. The administrator or supervisor must develop and implement appropriate policies and procedures. *Ford v. Breier,* 383 F. Supp. 505 (E.D. Wis. 1974);

Dewell v. Lawson, 89 F.2d 877 (10th Cir. 1974); *Bonsignore v. City of New York,* 521 F. Supp. 394 (S.D.N.Y. 1981).

Negligent Supervision

Whether the supervisor *knew or should have known* is the key. Failure to properly supervise employees can bring on a lawsuit for negligent supervision. *Marusa v. District of Columbia,* 484 F.2d 828 (D.C. Cir. 1973); *Brandon v. Holt,* 69 U.S. 464 (1985). If the supervisor is an "official policy-maker," then the employing municipality can also be held liable.

Parrish v. Luckie
963 F.2d 201 (8th Cir. 1992)

In *Parrish v. Luckie,* the city was liable for $200,000 for an officer's sexual assault and false arrest of a female, because the city had knowledge of the officer's propensity for violence and had failed to take any preventive action. This officer had been the subject of child abuse investigations on two previous occasions, being criminally charged once, but the police chief made no investigation into either incident. Furthermore, the record showed additional complaints against this officer, including one in which it was alleged that he repeatedly requested sexual favors from several store clerks. No action was taken on these complaints, and it was determined that investigators discouraged citizens from making complaints by telling them that if the investigator thought they were lying, they would be prosecuted and imprisoned. Also, no investigation would be initiated without a written complaint. The officer entered a guilty plea to a charge of first degree sexual assault, and in the Section 1983 action, $150,000 was awarded against the officer in his official capacity and $50,000 against the chief in his official capacity. Because neither award was against a defendant in his individual capacity, the city was liable for the entire $200,000 award.

Negligent Training

The local unit of government and the administrator or supervisor have an affirmative duty to train their employees. Failure to do so subjects the administrator or supervisor and the local unit of government to possible liability. *Owens v. Haas,* 601 F.2d 1242 (2d Cir. 1979).

In *Owens v. Haas,* the court clearly stated that gross negligence or a "deliberate indifference" to training and supervision would be a proper basis for liability. In fact, the two areas of negligence that have been the greatest sources for litigation under Section 1983 in recent years have been negligent supervision and negligent training.

Davis v. Mason County
49 CrL 1039 (1991)

In this case, a county sheriff was held to be the official policy-maker responsible for training his officers in the proper use of force, for the purposes of exposing the county to liability under Section 1983 for the deputies' unconstitutional use of excessive force.

Beverly v. Morris
470 F.2d 1356 (5th Cir. 1972)

In *Beverly v. Morris,* a Georgia police chief was held liable for improper performance of training and supervisory duties. A subordinate police officer had blackjacked the plaintiff. The liability resulted from the chief's failure to train the policeman.

Dewell v. Lawson
489 F.2d 877 (10th Cir. 1974)

In *Dewell,* the court held that an alleged failure to establish procedures and to train personnel to protect prisoners from medical injuries due to inattention established a cause of action (the prisoner was a diabetic who went into a coma and was permanently paralyzed as a result). However, the court did note that the standard of liability in a case alleging cruel and unusual punishment relating to a claimed omission of medical care is whether the plaintiff proves exceptional circumstances and the conduct is so grossly incompetent, inadequate, or excessive as to shock the conscience or to be intolerable to basic fairness.

City of Canton v. Harris
489 U.S. 378 (1989)

In *City of Canton v. Harris,* the U.S. Supreme Court held that ". . . the inadequacy of police training may serve as the basis for §1983 liability only where the failure to train in a relevant respect amounts to deliberate indifference to the constitutional rights of persons with whom the police come into contact" 489 U.S. 388-389. Of course, the Court was referring to the liability of the municipality and stated "[o]nly when a failure to train reflects a 'deliberate' or 'conscious' choice by the municipality can the failure be properly thought of as an actionable city 'policy' or 'custom' that is actionable under §1983" 489 U.S. at 389.

The standard of "deliberate indifference" by the municipality appears to be a very high standard that a plaintiff must overcome, but the manner in which the lower courts will interpret that phrase is yet to be seen. The Supreme Court has applied that term to a purposeful, malicious act, *Smith v. Wade,* 103 S. Ct. 1625 (1983), and has seemingly sanctioned a lower court's use of the term to describe an act of negligence. *Owens v. Haas,* 60 F.2d 1242 (2d Cir. 1979) *cert. denied,* 100 S. Ct. 483. Such a wide range of behaviors can fall into this standard that it is difficult to predict how the standard will be applied in future cases. How strictly this standard will be interpreted to restrict the liability of municipalities will be an area to watch in the 1990s, but it must be remembered that *Canton* dealt only with the issue of "failure to train."

There have been some cases that have ruled that even meeting state-mandated minimum standards of training may not, in some instances, be enough to avoid liability. Thus, failure to provide additional training over and above the required minimum has been deemed to be a "negligent failure to train" if it can also be shown (after *Canton*) that the failure amounts to "deliberate indifference" or a "conscious" choice by the municipality.

Popow v. City of Margate
476 F. Supp. 1237 (D.N.J. 1979)

In *Popow v. City of Margate,* a policeman shot at a fleeing suspect in a residential area at night. A man came out onto his porch to see what all the noise was and was killed by one of the shots. The police officers had received training in firearms that consisted of annual qualification, but had not received any training as to shooting moving targets, night firing, or use of firearms in a residential area, and the city of Margate was predominantly a residential community. The court held that even though the law enforcement officers involved had received the minimum training required under state law, additional training was necessary under the circumstances. Therefore, the court found that the city was negligent in its training.

Billings v. Vernal City
U.S. Dist. Utah, C77-0295 (1982)

In *Billings v. Vernal City,* a police officer who had been on the job for less than two weeks broke the plaintiff's arm while trying to arrest him (the arrest was illegal—the officer had no cause to even attempt to place the plaintiff under arrest). The plaintiff filed suit, alleging that the Chief of Police of Vernal City was "grossly" negligent because he failed to train the officer correctly. The allegation was based on the fact that the officer was on duty prior to completing the basic training required by the state. The city argued that this was allowable because Utah law allows a police officer to receive formal training "within 18 months" after beginning duty. The federal district judge stated that anyone who put such a police officer on duty for "one minute" was grossly negligent. Damages awarded: $12,500 against the Chief and the City, $11,000 against the Chief personally (punitive damages) $12,000 in costs, and $25,000 in attorney's fees.

In addition to subjecting subordinate personnel to training, the person responsible for the training must be absolutely sure that the training itself is done properly.

Sager v. City of Woodlawn Park
543 F. Supp. 282 (D. Colo. 1982)

In *Sager v. City of Woodlawn Park,* a suspect was accidentally killed by a police officer as the officer attempted to hold a gun on the suspect with one hand, and handcuff the suspect with the other hand. The officer's firearm discharged, killing the suspect. This technique had been shown in a training film seen by this officer; the training officer testified that the film was supposed to illustrate the *wrong* way to handcuff a prisoner. Unfortunately, no one told the training class that the film illustrated improper technique. The trial court rejected the argument that the death was not caused by the negligent training, stating that the chain of causation was sufficiently clear.

City of Oklahoma City v. Tuttle
728 F.2d 456 (10th Cir. 1984)

An Oklahoma City police officer fatally shot an individual in a street encounter. A Section 1983 suit was brought against the individual officer and against the city for its failure to train and supervise its officers in the use of force. A jury returned a verdict in favor of the officer but against the city and awarded $1.5 million in damages. On appeal, the city argued that a single incident of excessive force proven by the plaintiff was insufficient to establish a policy of negligent training. The Tenth Circuit disagreed, stating that the incident was "so plainly and grossly negligent that it spoke out very positively on the issue of lack of training." The United States Supreme Court reversed the Circuit Court, and the plurality decision stated that "[p]roof of a single incident of unconstitutional activity is not sufficient to impose liability under *Monell* unless proof of the incident includes proof that it was caused by an existing, unconstitutional municipal policy, which . . . can be attributed to a municipal policymaker" 471 U.S. at 823-824. The Court went on to say that otherwise, "the existence of the unconstitutional policy, and its origin, must be separately proved." 471 U.S. at 824. Because the instructions given to the jury allowed an inference without the proof, the case was remanded. As a result, it is still possible that a single incident can establish a "policy" of negligent training on the part of a municipality *if* evidence of the existence of an unconstitutional policy and a causal connection between the policy and the constitutional deprivation can be proved.

This entire area of failure to train or supervise is making supervisors and administrators directly liable for their omissions. It has been deemed that they have an affirmative duty to provide such training and supervision. This seems to be the most rapidly growing area of liability litigation. It is a form of vicarious liability that may extend beyond *respondeat superior*. Often this cause of action surfaces as a secondary Section 1983 action; however, it is becoming one of the most lucrative forms of litigation for the plaintiff.

It must be noted, however, that if the alleged deprivation involves only a property interest, and if there is an adequate remedy available to the plaintiff who alleges that his personal property has been destroyed, lost, or damaged by a person "acting under color of state law," a Section 1983 lawsuit may not be the proper action.

Parratt v. Taylor
451 U.S. 527 (1981)

A prison inmate ordered hobby materials valued at $23.50. The hobby materials were lost by prison officials and the inmate brought suit under Section 1983 to recover the cost of the lost items, alleging that the prison officials' conduct deprived him of property without due process of law in violation of the Fourteenth Amendment.

The United States Supreme Court noted that "[n]othing in the language of Section 1983 or its legislative history limits the statute solely to intentional deprivations of constitutional rights" 451 U.S. at 534. The Court went on to say that because the prison officials were state employees, they certainly acted under color of state law, and the only question to be determined was whether their actions deprived the plaintiff of any "right, privilege or immunity secured by the Constitution or laws of the United States" 451 U.S. at 534.

Because the plaintiff alleged that his Fourteenth Amendment rights were violated, the Court looked directly at the Fourteenth Amendment and concluded that:

> . . . petitioners [the prison officials] acted under color of state law; the hobby kit falls within the definition of property; and the alleged loss, even though negligently caused, amounted to a deprivation. Standing alone, however, these three elements do not establish a violation of the Fourteenth Amendment. Nothing in that amendment protects against all deprivations of life, liberty, or property by the state. The Fourteenth Amendment protects only against deprivations "without due process of law." . . . Our inquiry therefore must focus on whether the respondent [prison inmate] has suffered a deprivation without due process of law. In particular, we must decide whether the tort remedies which the State of Nebraska provides as a means of redress for property deprivation satisfies the requirements of procedural due process (451 U.S. 536-537).

After a lengthy review, the Court decided that the state did, indeed, provide for an adequate process that was available to the plaintiff. In short, the Court ruled that the actions complained of were not a violation of the Fourteenth Amendment. Therefore, Section 1983 was not a proper cause of action.

It is important to note, however, that the Court was clear in stating that negligence is a proper basis for a Section 1983 case.

> It is abundantly clear that one reason the legislation was passed was to afford a federal right in federal courts because, by reason of prejudice, passion, neglect, intolerance or otherwise, state laws might not be enforced and the claims of citizens to the enjoyment of rights, privileges and immunities guaranteed by the Fourteenth Amendment might be denied by the state agencies . . . . 81 S. Ct., at 480 (quoting from *Monroe v. Pape*).

Continuing to quote from *Monroe v. Pape,* the Court also was clear in stating that "Section 1983 should be read against the background of tort liability that makes a man responsible for the natural consequences of his actions . . . ." 81 S. Ct., at 494. The plaintiff "lost" in this case only because he failed to establish a "lack of due process" in the remedy available to recover the value of his lost property.

10 Personal Liability of Administrators and Supervisors

Generally, if a public administrator is sued he is sued in his official capacity and will not be personally liable. "State officers sued for damages in their official capacity are not 'persons' for purposes of the suit because they assume the identity of the government that employs them. By contrast, officers sued in their personal capacity come to the court as individuals." *Hafer v. Melo,* Slip Op. at p. 5 (1992). Thus, if certain conditions exist, a public administrator can be found *personally liable* for his acts or omissions. Although police chiefs generally are not vicariously liable in civil rights actions for their officers' unconstitutional acts, when they *knew or should have known* of the misconduct, and failed to act to prevent future harm, they may be directly liable for their own failures in training and supervising the offending subordinates.

McClelland v. Facteau
610 F.2d 693 (10th Cir. 1979)

A Section 1983 action was filed by Cecil McClelland against the Chief of the State Police Department and the Chief of the Farmington (New Mexico) City Police Department and three individual officers, alleging that his constitutional rights were violated during his arrest and custody. The chiefs did not personally participate in the alleged misconduct, but were charged with inadequate supervision and training of the other defendants and with failure to act in the face of knowledge of prior misconduct by those defendants.

McClelland was stopped by State Officer Facteau for speeding and was taken to the city jail. While in custody, McClelland was not allowed to make any phone calls, was questioned but not advised of his rights, and was made to lean against a wall where he was beaten and injured by Officer Facteau in the presence of two city police officers.

McClelland asserted that the police chiefs were directly liable through breach of their duty to properly train and supervise the subordinate officers (i.e., he was *not* arguing that the chiefs were liable under a *respondeat superior* theory). The court ruled that the chiefs could be held liable if the plaintiff could show that the defendants were adequately put on notice of prior misbehavior on the part of the subordinate officers and did nothing about it. (There were newspaper articles and affidavits indicating that it was well-known that rights were being violated in the city jail and by state police officer Facteau). The individual officers could also be held directly liable for their actions.

Brandon v. Allen
516 F. Supp. 1355 (W.D. Tenn. 1981)

In this case, two teenagers were parked in a well-known "lovers lane," when a pickup truck stopped near them. The driver identified himself as a police officer and showed them an official police identification card. He was, in fact, a police officer, but was off-duty at the time. Officer Allen ordered the male out of the car and struck him with his fist and stabbed him with a knife, and attempted to break into the car where the female was seated. The young male jumped back into the car and quickly drove away and Officer Allen fired a shot at them with his police revolver. Both teenagers were seriously injured by the shattered glass from the shot-out windshield and required plastic surgery. Officer Allen was found guilty of criminal charges stemming from this incident and was sent to prison. The Director of the Police Department was also named in this Section 1983 action.

Even though Allen was off duty, the court ruled that his use of his police identification and service revolver were acts done under color of state law. The court also found that Officer Allen's reputation as a "mental case" was widespread among the city police officers, and none wished to ride in the same squad car with him. In addition, at least two formal complaints had been filed with the Memphis Police Department concerning Officer Allen.

The District Court ruled that the Director failed to take proper action to become informed of Allen's dangerous propensities by failing to even review the disciplinary records of officers when he became Police Director. The court called the Director's "unjustified inaction" the cause of the plaintiffs' damages and injuries and held the police department liable. The Court of Appeals reversed, stating that the Director "acted in good faith" and therefore was immune from liability. On January 21, 1985, the United States Supreme Court reversed the Court of Appeals, stating that it was clear that the Director had been sued in his official capacity, not as an individual, and that was tantamount to being a suit against the city of Memphis. Because under *Owen* the city cannot claim a "good faith" defense, the city of Memphis was ordered to pay the damages awarded to the plaintiffs. (*Brandon v. Holt*, 469 U.S. 464, 105 S. Ct. 873 (1985); see also *Hafer v. Melo* and *McClelland v. Facteau, supra.*)

Payment of Attorney's Fees

Liability to pay all of the plaintiff's attorney's fees can also be personal. A state or local official who infringes on an individual's constitutional rights in the sincere belief that his conduct is proper may later find himself personally liable not only for damages but for attorney's fees as well. The U.S. Supreme Court has stated that ". . . state officials, sued in their individual capacities are 'persons' within the meaning of §1983. The Eleventh Amendment does not bar such suits nor are state officers absolutely immune from personal liability under §1983 solely by virtue of the 'official' nature of their acts." *Hafer v. Melo,* Slip Op. at p. 9. If the official is held liable in his individual capacity in a Section 1983 action and is found to have acted in objective bad faith, then he may also be required to pay punitive damages as well as his opponent's attorney's fees under the 1976 Civil Rights Attorney's Fee Award Act, 42 U.S.C. Section 1988.

Elements of a Personal Liability Lawsuit

An administrator or supervisor can be *personally* liable for the actions of subordinates if he or she:

1. knew or should have known

2. of the existence of a pattern of gross abuse, and

3. did nothing after having such knowledge.

There are two exceptions to the "pattern" requirement:

1. If there was a disregard of "clearly established law—*McNamara v. Moody, supra.*

2. If the failure to supervise or the lack of proper training programs was so severe as to constitute "gross negligence" or "deliberate indifference" to plaintiff's constitutional rights—*Owens v. Haas,* 601 F.2d 1242 (2d Cir. 1979), *cert. denied,* 100 S. Ct. 483.

Under those conditions, the administrator or supervisor will be held liable. Further, a state or local official who infringes on an individual's constitutional rights in the sincere belief that his conduct is proper may later find himself *personally* liable not only for damages but for attorneys' fees as well. If the official is held liable in his individual capacity in a Section 1983 action and is found to have acted in "objective bad faith," then he may also be required to pay his opponent's attorneys' fees under 42 U.S.C. Section 1988.

If the administrator himself sets the policy that is considered the cause of the deprivation committed by his subordinate, the administrator will be held directly liable and, as an official of the employing unit of local government, his policies may well be considered to be the official policies of the local government, thereby making the local government liable under the rationale of *Monell.*

Black v. Stephens
662 F.2d 181 (3d Cir. 1981)

Elwood and Joyce Black filed a Section 1983 civil rights action against Chief of Police Carson Gable, Detective Wayne Stephens, and the City of Allentown, Pennsylvania as a result of a confrontation between the Blacks and Detective Stephens.

The Blacks stopped for a red light, and Stephens, on duty as a plainclothes detective, pulled behind them in an unmarked patrol car. According to the Blacks, when the traffic light changed, they proceeded through the intersection and Stephens suddenly passed them by crossing the double yellow lines. At the next intersection, Stephens jumped out of his car and, without identifying himself, approached the Blacks' car and started screaming that Black was a "rotten driver." Black put his car in reverse and then tried to drive around Stephens. At this point Stephens pulled out his service revolver and aimed it directly at Black's head. Stephens screamed that Black had driven over his foot and threatened to shoot if Black did not move the car. Black testified that the car was nowhere near Stephens' foot, but he backed up and drove around the right of Stephens' vehicle.

About two miles down the road, the Blacks encountered a police roadblock. They were stopped and arrested for aggravated assault. Stephens' version of the story was quite different, but there was general agreement as to what happened next.

Stephens filed a criminal complaint for aggravated assault against Black. Two days later, Black registered a complaint about Stephens' behavior with the chief of police, but was informed that in accordance with police department policy, no investigation of Stephens' conduct would commence until the charge against Black was resolved. After the chief informed Stephens that Black had made a complaint of use of excessive force, Stephens filed three additional charges against Black. These three charges were all dismissed, and Black was found guilty of simple assault, which was reversed on appeal.

The court stated that while there was conflicting testimony as to what actually had happened that there was "more than enough evidence from which the jury could find that Stephens' actions deprived the Blacks of their constitutional rights" 662 F.2d at 188. Elwood Black testified that his car was never on detective Stephens' foot and that he did not provoke Stephens to draw his gun. In addition, an expert witness testified that the Blacks' car weighed 5,160 pounds and that 1,340 pounds of pressure would be exerted by the left front tire that was allegedly on Stephens' foot. Yet the physician who examined Stephens immediately after the incident testified that there were no contusions, lacerations or visible signs of any injury to Stephens' toe, and the x-rays for fractures and dislocations were also negative. The court stated that while there were conflicting versions of the incident, "we cannot hold that the jury's findings of liability was irrational . . ." 662 F.2d at 188.

Gable, the chief of police, was held liable because the jury found that he promulgated and implemented a police regulation that caused detective Stephens to file three unwarranted charges against the Blacks. In addition, the jury found that Gable had a policy of encouraging members of the Allentown police department to use excessive force in the performance of their duties and that this policy was the proximate cause of Stephens' use of excessive force against the Blacks. The court found evidence to support this finding and stated:

> Chief Gable's policy concerning the use of excessive force ensured that a citizen's complaint about excessive force never went into a police officer's permanent personnel file

> .... Indeed, such a complaint could only get into an officer's record if the officer put it there himself. Although Chief Gable stated that he was in exclusive control of police discipline, he testified that he never initiated a disciplinary action against an officer based solely on his evaluation of the officer's use of force. . . . In addition, . . . he added that Officer Stephens would probably not have been promoted to detective if he had been the type of officer who backed down when force was involved . . . . Finally, Chief Gable stated that any officer "worth his salt" would use force every week of his career because very few arrests are made without it . . . 662 F.2d at 190-191.

The court went on to state that Gable may fairly be said to represent "official policy" for the City of Allentown, and thus, under *Monell*, the municipality was also liable. The jury awarded the Blacks $35,000 in compensatory and punitive damages against all three defendants (Detective Stephens, Chief Gable, and the city).

The chief was also liable individually. If a plaintiff can establish supervisory negligence or indifference, the supervisor can then be held liable; if the supervisor is a "policymaker" then a suit against him in his official capacity can also be filed.

11 Personnel Issues Under Section 1983

Criminal justice practitioners, usually the defendants in civil liability suits, are, in increasing numbers, themselves bringing actions against their employers to settle grievances. Two Milwaukee County, Wisconsin, sheriff's deputies were attacked in their patrol car by a prisoner who had hidden a gun, keys, and cash in a body cavity and took them out during a trip from the Milwaukee County jail to the Dane County jail in Madison. The deputies claimed that their rights were violated because of the recklessness of Milwaukee County and several individuals named as defendants. A jury awarded the two deputies $5.3 million (*Crime Control Digest,* 2/17/92, p. 3).

The City of Detroit agreed to pay a total of $975,000 to all Detroit police officers, ending a lawsuit of more than four years, that challenged the constitutionality of Detroit's random drug testing of its police officers. The settlement did not do away with the random testing, but did eliminate strip searches and other aspects of the process (*Crime Control Digest,* 12/21/92, p. 3).

Although there are numerous civil rights statutes that prohibit discrimination in hiring, promoting, and firing on the basis of race, color, creed, sex, or age, Section 1983 can also be utilized in the personnel area. As noted earlier, a supervisor or administrator can be sued if he or she is deemed to have been "negligent" in the hiring, assignment, retention, entrustment, direction, supervision, or training of subordinate personnel. In addition, such supervisors or administrators can be sued by subordinate personnel if the administrator or supervisor is deemed to have violated the subordinate's rights when failing to promote, in disciplinary actions, and in the firing process. In fact, Section 1983 can even be utilized in some circumstances for improperly failing to hire a person.

Non-Hire

It is possible that Section 1983 can be used as the basis for a lawsuit by someone who applies for an open position and is not hired (other civil rights statutes also come into play here). The agency or the administrator or supervisor responsible for the hiring decision must be able to show that the hiring decision was not based on race, color, sex, creed, and so forth, but that the individual was unqualified for some other reason. If testing is part of the hiring decision, it must be shown that the tests utilized were: (1) job-related, (2) validated, (3) free from "inherent bias," (4) properly administered, and (5) properly graded.

Failure to establish any of the above criteria will be deemed a proper cause of action for a Section 1983 lawsuit. The failure to document the above criteria will be viewed by the courts as being *prima facie* evidence that the individual's Fourteenth Amendment rights were violated.

Non-Promotion

Essentially, the same standards that apply to the hiring or non-hiring decision apply to the promotion/non-promotion decision. The promotion decision must be free from racial, religious, and sexual discrimination. Again, if tests are utilized in the promotion process, it must be shown that the tests are: (1) job-related, (2) validated, (3) free from inherent bias, (4) properly administered, and (5) properly (fairly, objectively) graded. There must be adequate documentation to support the decision.

Failure to Warn of Hazardous Work Conditions

In *Collins v. City of Harker Heights, Texas,* 112 S. Ct. 1061 (1992), the Supreme Court held that while a city's actions may possibly be actionable under state law, a city does not violate Section 1983 by failing to train or warn employees about known hazards in the workplace. The Court stated that Section 1983 does not provide a remedy for abuses that do not violate federal law, but the Court did find that an employee could have a valid claim under some circumstances (*Police Misconduct and Civil Rights Law Report,* May-June 1992, p. 176).

Discipline/Firing

A federal appeals court in San Francisco ruled on September 17, 1992, that the constitutional rights of a Los Angeles police officer were violated when he was fired in 1986 for refusing to take a drug test. The court ruled that he could not be forced to take a drug test unless he was suspected of using narcotics, and it upheld a jury award of $150,000. The officer already had been reinstated and paid one and one-half years' back pay by an arbitrator who found that the firing had violated his union contract (*Crime Control Digest*, 9/28/92, p. 7).

In order to sustain a disciplinary action taken because of off-duty activities, it is generally required that there be a clear showing that an employee's off-duty activities adversely affect his job performance.

Swope v. Bratton
541 F. Supp. 99 (W.D. Ark. 1982)

In *Swope v. Bratton*, a police officer was disciplined as a result of a private relationship with a female employee of the police department of which the police chief disapproved. The Court held that in disciplining the officer, the police department violated his constitutional right to privacy under the Fourteenth Amendment. That is, in the absence of a nexus between personal, off-duty activities and poor job performance, inquiry into these activities violates the constitutionally protected right of privacy.

If an employee refuses to conform to regulations, it must be shown that there is a strong governmental interest in the regulation that outweighs the employee's constitutionally protected interests.

Kelley v. Johnson
96 S. Ct. 1440 (1976)

In *Kelley*, the county's determination that a hair grooming regulation should be enacted was related to the county's legitimate interest in the appearance of its police officers, and therefore outweighed the employee's claimed liberty interest in freedom to choose a hairstyle.

Leonard v. City of Columbus
705 F.2d 1299 (11th Cir. 1983)

In this case, black police officers removed the American flag from their uniforms to protest what they perceived as racially discriminatory practices by the city. They were dismissed and brought suit, alleging infringement of their First Amendment rights. The Court found that the flag incident was a substantial factor in their dismissals; that the employees' interest in free speech was substantial in that it was a protest of racial discrimination and was of interest to the community-at-large; and that the governmental interest in having the flags worn was weak.

Although common practice in many jurisdictions, the U.S. Supreme Court has ruled that employees cannot be dismissed because of their political affiliation or their lack of overt political support for the hiring authority unless they are considered to be a "confidential" or "policy making" employee.

Elrod v. Burns
427 U.S. 347 (1975)

In *Elrod v. Burns*, newly elected Sheriff Elrod discharged the plaintiffs solely because they were not affiliated with or sponsored by the Democratic Party. The Supreme Court stated that the practice of patronage dismissals violated the plaintiffs' First and Fourteenth Amendment rights, and ruled that the Court of Appeals was correct in issuing an injunction prohibiting the sheriff from firing the plaintiffs. Justices Stewart and Blackmun joined the plurality's judgment but stated that "[t]he single substantive question involved in this case is whether a nonpolicymaking, nonconfidential government employee can be discharged or threatened with discharge from a job that he is satisfactorily performing." 427 U.S. at 375. The answer was, he cannot.

Branti v. Finkel
445 U.S. 507 (1979)

In *Branti*, respondents, both Republicans, brought suit in Federal District Court to enjoin petitioner, a Democrat, who had recently been appointed Public Defender of Rockland County, N.Y., by the Democrat-dominated county legislature, from discharging respondents from their positions as Assistant Public Defenders. Finding that the respondents had been satisfactorily performing their jobs and had been selected for termination solely because they were Republicans and that an assistant public defender is neither a policymaker nor a confidential employee, the District Court held that petitioner could not terminate respondents' employment. The Court of Appeals affirmed.

The United States Supreme Court stated:

> If the First Amendment protects a public employee from discharge based on what he has said, it must also protect him from discharge based on what he believes. Under this line of analysis, unless the government can demonstrate "an over- riding interest, . . . of vital importance," . . . requiring that a person's private beliefs conform to those of the hiring authority, his beliefs cannot be the sole basis for depriving him of continued public employment. 445 U.S., at 515-516.

The Court went on to admit that it is not always easy to determine whether a position is one in which political affiliation is a legitimate factor to be considered. "Under some circumstances, a position may be appropriately considered political even though it is neither confidential nor policymaking in character . . . . In sum, the ultimate inquiry is not whether the label 'policymaker' or 'confidential' fits a particular position; rather, the question is whether the hiring authority can demonstrate that party affiliation is an appropriate requirement for the effective performance of the public office involved." 445 U.S. at 518.

In this case, the Court determined that the primary, if not the only, responsibility of an assistant public defender is to represent individual citizens in controversy with the State. "Accordingly, the entry of an injunction against termination of respondents' employment on purely political grounds was appropriate and the judgment of the Court of Appeals is *Affirmed.*" 445 U.S. 519-520.

It would seem clear, then, that a sheriff (or any other hiring authority) cannot fire an employee at "his pleasure" despite the almost universal belief that he can. A "policymaker" or "confidential" employee has no rights to employment and certainly can be terminated at the pleasure of the hiring authority. All other employees, however, have liberty interests and possibly property interests in their employment. Therefore, the requirements of due process must be met in order to terminate an employee, even when the termination is for cause.

The cases above also clearly indicate that if the sheriff, chief of police, or other public administrator is not extremely careful when making decisions concerning discipline or firing, he or she will not only lose a great deal of money but may also lose a great deal of authority in the running of his or her department.

Due Process Requirements

As indicated in *Owen v. City of Independence,* 55 U.S. 622 (1980) and the cases previously cited in this chapter, it is mandatory that a proper hearing be granted to an employee to appeal hiring, promotion, discipline, and firing decisions. Today, it is not enough to simply state that the person was not doing his or her job or that he or she was an embarrassment to the department or agency. In order to legally fire someone, the agency (through the administrator or supervisor who actually does the firing) must, as a minimum, be able to show:

1. There are substantive reasons for deciding to fire the employee;

2. The agency has established a "proper procedure" to follow in all firings;

3. The established procedure was followed in the instant case, brought about by the substantive reasons cited; and

4. It must be shown by specific acts that the conduct had an adverse impact on the department or on the public in order to "justify" a firing for behavioral or "conduct" reasons.

Exhaustion of Administrative Remedies

It is not necessary that an employee exhaust his administrative remedies prior to filing a Section 1983 lawsuit.

Patsy v. Board of Regents
102 S. Ct. 2557 (1982)

In this case, the plaintiff alleged that even though she was qualified and received uniformly excellent performance evaluations from her supervisors, she had been rejected for more than thirteen positions at Florida International University (FIU). She claimed that FIU unlawfully filled positions through intentional discrimination on the basis of race and sex. The Board argued that the plaintiff had not yet exhausted all of her administrative remedies on the campus and before the Board itself. The Supreme Court ruled that she was not required to exhaust those remedies but could pursue her cause of action directly under Section 1983

Thus, in the personnel area, the plaintiff need not exhaust the administrative remedies that are available, but rather can proceed directly to a Section 1983 action.

Therefore, it would seem that in the personnel area, Section 1983 is becoming a force with which all criminal justice agencies and all criminal justice practitioners who have supervisory responsibility will have to deal. It seems likely that there will be more suits filed by criminal justice personnel against their employing agencies as these personnel become better educated with regard to Section 1983 actions. It is somewhat ironic that the personnel who could find themselves defendants in Section 1983 actions are using the same legal theories to challenge their own treatment. The employing agencies that are being attacked with Section 1983 actions for the conduct of their employees are also being sued by the employees themselves.

Given the acceptance today that supervisory negligence can result in both "official" and "individual" liability when a suit is filed against a subordinate, it is extremely likely that suits alleging supervisory negligence or "indifference" will continue to be a ripe area for criminal justice practitioners to explore. This seems to be a "double-barreled" assault on criminal justice supervisors, administrators, and hiring authorities. Section 1983 is not the cause of concern here, because, as the Supreme Court has said, "[b]y its terms, of course, the statute creates no substantive rights, it merely provides remedies for deprivations of rights established elsewhere" *Oklahoma City v. Tuttle,* 471 U.S. 808 at 816 (1985). It is the deprivations of constitutional rights of criminal justice practitioners that should be the concern, and when these deprivations occur, criminal justice practitioners certainly should be able to redress those wrongdoings just as every other citizen can.

12 Defenses and Lawsuit Prevention Strategies

Some officials, such as judges, prosecutors, parole officials, and legislators, enjoy absolute immunity from liability with regard to their official duties and functions. Other officials, such as executive and administrative officials, are only protected by *qualified, good faith immunity*.

Qualified Immunity

Executive and administrative officials enjoy *qualified*, or *good faith* immunity, which is an affirmative defense that must be pleaded by a defendant. The defendant must demonstrate to the satisfaction of the jury that he acted in good faith and that his conduct was reasonable. This defense is available to:

1. Police officers. As members of the executive branch of government, they enjoy good faith immunity from prosecution. *Pierson v. Ray,* 386 U.S. 547 (1967); *Monroe v. Pape,* 365 U.S. 167 (1961). Much of their conduct is discretionary, and the courts realize that honest mistakes can and will be made from time to time. It is the overzealous conduct, not done in good faith, without regard for individual rights that generally results in damage awards and the adverse publicity that is seen each day in the newspaper, on television, and in the courtrooms.

2. Prison officials have qualified, good faith immunity from prosecution if they have not violated "clearly established" rights of inmates. *Procunier v. Navarette,* 434 U.S. 555 (1978).

3. Judges, prosecutors, and probation and parole officers enjoy absolute immunity for all their official judicial or quasi-judicial actions, but enjoy only qualified, good faith immunity for non-official acts.

4. School officials: As stated by the United States Supreme Court:

> [A] school board member is not immune from liability for damages under Section 1983 if he knew or reasonably should have known that the action he took within the sphere of official responsibility would violate the constitutional rights of the student affected, or if he took the action with the malicious intention to cause a deprivation of constitutional rights or other injury to the student." *Wood v. Strickland,* 420 U.S. 308 at 322 (1975).

5. Administrators of state mental hospitals have "qualified" immunity, *O'Connor v. Donaldson,* 422 U.S. 563 (1975). In view of the difficult decisions that must be made by such persons, they will be protected by good faith immunity as long as they exercise professional judgment and have not departed substantially from accepted professional practice or standards. *Youngberg v. Romero,* 102 S. Ct. 2452 (1982).

6. A governor, the president of a state university, and officials of a state national guard have been held to have qualified immunity in *Scheuer v. Rhodes,* 416 U.S. 232 (1974).

Inasmuch as the vast majority of criminal justice practitioners are in the executive branch of government, the qualified, good faith immunity defense is available to them. Again, however, it must be stressed that the qualified, good faith immunity is an *affirmative* defense that must be pleaded and proven to the satisfaction of the fact-finder (judge or jury); it is not an automatic defense.

The "Good Faith" Test

In *Wood v. Strickland, supra,* the Supreme Court set an objective test and a subjective test to determine whether the defendant acted in good faith. The Court modified that test in *Harlow v. Fitzgerald,* 102 S. Ct. 2727 (1982), stating that:

> [G]overnment officials performing discretionary functions generally are shielded from liability for civil damages insofar as their conduct does not violate clearly established statutory or constitutional rights of which a reasonable person would have known . . . . Reliance on the objective reasonableness of an official's conduct, as measured by reference to clearly established law, should . . . permit the resolution of many insubstantial claims on summary judgement. 102 S. Ct. 2727 at 2738-39.

Whether *Harlow* eliminates malicious intent as a factor is unclear. The Court stated that "bare allegations of malice" will no longer suffice to subject government officials to either the costs of trial or the burdens of far-reaching discovery. However, it could be argued that perhaps a detailed or "substantial" allegation would suffice. At any rate, the subjective test has been dropped, and now the test is an objective one: did the official act in a manner that violated clearly established law? If so, he or she did not act in good faith.

An "Acceptable Beginning"

If it can be established that the agency or administrator discovered the problem that led to or caused a deprivation of rights, or was seen as likely to cause a deprivation, and steps had been taken to correct that problem prior to a lawsuit being filed, the agency or administrator can argue that an "acceptable beginning" has been made in correcting the problem and that the actions were not taken as a result of the lawsuit. If action is started (and documented prior to a lawsuit being filed, the courts are more likely to allow the opportunity to bring about the needed change (see *Salinas v. Breier,* 517 F. Supp. 1272 (E.D. Wis. 1981) and *Ford v. Breier,* 383 F. Supp. 505 (E.D. Wis. 1974)). This is an especially important defense for administrators being sued for vicarious liability.

Valid Authority

It is also a valid defense to plead that the actions complained of were based upon what reasonably appeared to be valid authority. As with the other defenses, however, it must be proven to the satisfaction of the jury and is not automatic.

Invalid Defenses

Conduct that is clearly unreasonable or outrageous negates all of the valid defenses. *Monroe v. Pape; Owens v. Haas, etc.* Even if unintentional (i.e., negligent actions), such conduct will negate any claim of an otherwise valid defense. Clearly outrageous conduct may also subject the officer or officials to punitive damages or even to criminal liability, especially if a death or serious injury occurred. See *Brandon v. Allen*, 16 F. Supp. 1355 (W.D. Tenn. 1981) and *Domashewsky v. Sierociuk*, No. 84L-24504, Cook County Circuit Court, Ill.; 34 ATLA L. Rep. 336 (Nov. 1991) as examples.

Lack of Funding

Lack of funding is not a defense. That is, to claim that the city, county, or state simply does not have the money to provide constitutional police departments and jails is an invalid defense. The courts are not going to allow a "budgetary" defense and will require that non-constitutionally required programs be cut in order to fund constitutionally required standards. In short, the state, county, or city will have to find a way to raise the funds or do without, as indicated by the following:

> If the State cannot obtain the resources to detain persons awaiting trial in accordance with minimum constitutional standards, then the State will simply not be permitted to detain such persons (*Hamilton v. Love*, 328 F. Supp. 1182 at 1184).
>
> Let there be no mistake in the matter; that obligation of the respondents [government] to eliminate existing unconstitutionalities does not depend upon what the legislature may do, or upon what the Governor may do, or indeed upon what the respondents may actually be able to accomplish. If Arkansas is going to operate a penitentiary system,

it is going to have to be a system that is countenanced by the Constitution of the United States. (*Finney v. Arkansas*, 505 F.2d 194 at 199 (8th Cir. 1974).

The United States Supreme Court upheld this concept in *Hutto v. Finney*, 437 U.S. 678 (1978).

Although there are "defenses" available, objective good faith may be difficult to establish—especially in the face of what appears to the jury to be unreasonable conduct. Also, to establish an acceptable beginning, non-negligent supervision, training, direction, or assignment requires *substantial documentation*—documentation that most criminal justice agencies are unable to produce. In short, it may be quite difficult to defend a properly formed cause of action under Section 1983 even if the act was done in good faith or in a non-negligent manner. Even though most suits have a strong factual basis, it is evident that many suits can be brought against conscientious criminal justice practitioners who were doing their best and who later are unable to adequately defend themselves.

Obviously, the best defense is to *prevent* the suit from being filed in the first place. That is, a proactive approach to prevent Section 1983 lawsuits appears to be a better course of action than trying to defend oneself after a suit has been filed.

Lawsuit Prevention

There are several general principles that should be followed in order to prevent lawsuits. Most of these principles may appear to be self-evident or even simplistic, but they are often ignored.

Know the Law

The courts presume that persons in positions of responsibility know the law pertaining to their duties. The courts often seem especially to presume that law enforcement officers know, or should know, the law. Thus, in a very real sense, ignorance of the law is no excuse, and it certainly is not a valid defense.

Policies and Procedures

It is also necessary to develop, maintain and follow written policies and procedures. However, if an agency does have policies and procedures (and it must), it has to be absolutely sure to follow those policies and procedures to the letter. If it can be shown that an agency has no policy, the agency is in trouble; if it can be shown that an agency has a policy but did not follow it, the agency is in greater trouble.

Training

As previously noted, negligent failure to properly train is a valid cause of action under Section 1983. Therefore, all personnel must be properly trained in all aspects of their job. As seen in *Billings, supra,* and *City of Margate, supra,* merely meeting state-mandated minimum standards may not be enough; the training provided must be correct, *Sager v. City of Woodlawn Park, supra;* and simply attending a "training" session will not be enough. Rather, it must now be shown that:

1. the training was necessary as validated by a task analysis;

2. the persons conducting the training were, in fact, qualified to conduct such training;

3. the training did, in fact, take place and was properly conducted and documented;

4. the training was "state-of-the-art" and up-to- date;

5. adequate measures of mastery of the subject matter can be documented;

6. those who did not satisfactorily "learn" in the training session have received additional training and now have mastery of the subject matter; and

7. close supervision exists to monitor and continually evaluate the trainee's progress.

In short, the courts are now making it clear that it is no longer enough to say that an agency provides training; the agency must be able to prove it.

Supervision

As pointed out above, after providing proper training, it is also necessary to insure that close supervision exists. It is now clearly established that supervisors can and are being held liable for the acts of their subordinates. Whether the supervisor "knew or should have known" is usually the key. Failure to supervise properly can create liability for negligent supervision. *Marusa v. District of Columbia, supra.* If deliberate indifference after full knowledge of a pattern of gross abuse can be established, liability will attach and can be passed on to the employing municipality or county if the failure to supervise amounts to deliberate indifference as stated in *City of Canton v. Harris.*

Documentation

Proper documentation is the key to lawsuit prevention. Basically, courts now rule that *if it is not documented, it did not happen* (See, for example, *Whiteley v. Warden,* 401 U.S. 560 (1971). One thing is certain—*when a mistake occurs, someone will be held responsible* (guilty or not); and it is equally certain that the *one with the least documentation will be the one held responsible.* Protect yourself by documenting all training and supervisory activities.

Specific Proactive Principles

Evaluation

It is necessary that an objective evaluation of the current situation be made. An agency (and individual administrators and supervisors) must be honest and ask the tough questions to determine potential liability. The answers to those questions must be objectively evaluated by using both state and federal standards. The fewer questions that can be answered, the less satisfactory the answers are, the less information there is that can be documented, the further away from state and federal standards the agency (and administrator or supervisor) is, the greater the potential for liability.

Management and Money

Having completed the evaluation to determine the potential for liability lawsuits being filed against the agency (or yourself, as an administrator or supervisor), the problem areas identified should be divided into two categories—Management and Money. That is, determine which problems can be solved by instituting management changes, often without the expenditure of any funds, and which problems will require additional funding to solve.

Prioritize

After evaluating the current situation and identifying which potential liability areas are management problems and which are related to funding, it is necessary to determine which problems are the most likely to bring about a lawsuit if not corrected. In this way, the greatest needs (i.e., greatest liability risks) are identified and can be addressed first.

Master Plan

Having evaluated the potential for liability and having determined in which areas the liability can be reduced or removed by changes in procedure and management, it is necessary to set up a master plan to correct all of the deficiencies. This master plan will assist you in determining:

1. What is to be done; and

2. When it will be done.

Implementation

Obviously, the final step is to implement the master plan (what the courts would view as an "acceptable beginning"). Having taken these steps, the agency (administrator or supervisor) will have—at the very least—have avoided liability at their level of the organization.

Summary

Criminal justice practitioners and agencies must take a proactive-prevention stance. The advantages to undertaking the proactive-prevention orientation are certain. Even if mistakes are made and litigation is not avoided, the process itself may be sufficient to establish a good faith defense for supervisors and others. Likewise, if the lawsuit is seeking major injunctive relief, the efforts being made may constitute an "acceptable beginning" to remedying the problem, allowing the court to delay any action while progress is being made (*Ford v. Breier, supra*).

Thus, there are basically two rules to follow if you do not have control over financial matters:

1. Avoid liability at your level of the administration.

2. Document everything. If it is not documented, it did not happen.

Likewise, if you are the holder of the purse strings, there are two rules to follow:

1. Make an "acceptable beginning" prior to the lawsuit being filed to show your good faith in attempting to correct the deficiencies.

2. Provide documentation for all activities.

Those intimately involved with the criminal justice system know that, historically, the system has been reactive in its orientation and operations. State legislatures, as well as city and county councils, have never provided full funding for the system; therefore, recruitment procedures, training programs, and supervision have all suffered. All of these conditions must change. Given the operation of most criminal justice agencies today, the potential for successful defense of a legitimate Section 1983 lawsuit is very difficult at best, except for obviously frivolous cases. Preventing the lawsuit from being filed in the first place may be the only viable solution.

13 Trends

There seems to be no end to the ever-increasing number of Section 1983 lawsuits filed against criminal justice practitioners, and because the trends have remained constant for the past several years, there is no reason to believe that there will be a slowdown anytime soon. There are simply too many developments that seem to encourage Section 1983 actions. A discussion of some of these developments follows.

The Demise of the Exclusionary Rule

The United States Supreme Court has created several exceptions to the exclusionary rule. Although the exclusionary rule may well have had some deterrent effect on law enforcement conduct in the areas of investigation, interrogation, and identification, it is debatable whether it had any meaningful deterrent effect in the area of search and seizure. Nevertheless, with the growing list of exceptions being made to the rule by the Supreme Court (for example, the good faith exception of *United States v. Leon,* 104 S. Ct. 3405 (1984); the "inevitable discovery" exception of *Nix v. Williams,* 104 S. Ct. 2501 (1984), and the public safety exception to *Miranda* set forth in *New York v. Quarles,* 104 S. Ct. 2626 (1984)), the *perception* is that new means of deterrence must be found in order to effectively deter and control law enforcement conduct. Obviously, the filing of Section 1983 lawsuits is being viewed as one of those means.

Uncertainty and Continued Change in Section 1983 Applicability

In any area of the law in which rapid change and uncertainty exist, there will be a multitude of lawsuits filed. Under such conditions, the only way in which issues can be adequately dealt with is through actual litigation. Unfortunately, mixed signals are now being sent as the various federal circuit courts hand down conflicting opinions, and the Supreme Court sometimes adds to the confusion. The most recent cases *seem* to indicate some consistency by the Court, but there is still no distinct pattern in the decisions; the Court seemingly closes one door or limits liability in one case only to open a new door or expand liability in the next case. The situation is not a new one; it occurs in all new areas of litigation. Nevertheless, it is not comforting to realize that this extremely important area of the law is far from being clearly established.

Lawyers Becoming More Knowledgeable About Section 1983

The vast majority of attorneys rarely, if ever, engage in federal litigation. As a result, only a few are truly knowledgeable about federal law and only a small percentage of these attorneys practice in the civil rights arena. However, there have been so many cases reported that Section 1983 has become a popular issue of discussion in law journals, trade papers, and other legal publications. Lawyers who had not even heard of Section 1983 a few years ago are beginning to study its applications, and seminars and workshops on the subject are being held all around the country. As more and more attorneys begin to become familiar with and understand Section 1983 or simply desire to "test the waters" in an exciting and new area, more and more cases will be filed.

Population Migration and Changes in Values

Certain areas of the country, such as the sun belt and the rural areas, have for the most part been free of large numbers of Section 1983 cases. This has, unfortunately, brought about a false feeling of security on the part of many criminal justice practitioners in those areas. "It won't happen here because it only happens in the big cities," and "it goes against our tradition" are really no more than expressions of wishful thinking. It is clear that the question no longer is if there will be a suit, but rather, when there will be a suit. As industry continues to move into the sun belt and into other predominantly rural areas, it brings not only technology and jobs, but people as well. These people may bring with them different value systems and different ways of life; they may be more used to litigation as a means of solving problems, and therefore be more likely to bring suit against the sheriff or police officer. At the same time, the values of the natives of the area are also undergoing change. Even though the institution of law enforcement is still highly respected, in some cases, individual law enforcement officers are not. Ten years ago the sheriff or any of his deputies or any police officer would usually not be challenged, no matter what he did or said. Today, that simply is not true. No longer is it felt that "nothing can be done" or "we can't do anything about it." It is no longer considered "wrong" to sue the sheriff or the police department. These changes, brought about through evolution and migration, are expected to continue.

The Growing Weight of Precedent

In many regions, federal judges have seemingly been reluctant to apply Section 1983 except in the most extreme cases. Some would classify these judges as being more conservative than the majority of federal judges who, as a group, are usually considered to be more liberal than state court judges, and more concerned for individual rights. Whether any of those observations are true, the fact is that the weight of precedent in the area of Section 1983 litigation is compelling judges to apply Section 1983 with more vigor or risk being overturned by the Court of Appeals or the Supreme Court. It is an area of the law that can no longer be ignored.

Abuses Continue

Unfortunately, the main reason Section 1983 litigation will not go away is simply because criminal justice practitioners continue to engage in conduct that results in litigation. The newspapers, as well as the court dockets, are filled with allegations of outrageous conduct, negligent conduct, and indifferent conduct on the part of criminal justice practitioners. The following reports illustrate this point: Correctional officers conduct 10 searches of an inmate's cell over a 19-day period, apparently because the inmate reported another officer's misconduct (*Scher v. Engelke, The Law Officer's Bulletin,* September, 1991); in New York City, four white police officers, including a sergeant and a lieutenant, were convicted in 1985 of assault, collusion, and official misconduct for participating in repeated acts of torture—using stun guns to repeatedly shock black and Latino arrestees (*Police Misconduct and Civil Rights Law Report,* January-February, 1990); in Chicago, the evidence of repeated acts of police torture is so widespread that a federal jury found in a Section 1983 trial that the police department had "a *de facto* policy, practice and custom of police abuse and torture" (*Police Misconduct and Civil Rights Law Report,* January-February 1990, p. 8). Even a review of the cases summarized in this handbook makes an objective person wonder how and why such persons become criminal justice practitioners. The cases smack of outright brutality and stupidity more than honest mistakes or even "overzealous" enforcement. While only the most outrageous cases are the ones that come to light, and while these cases represent the smallest minority of criminal justice practitioner activity, they do, nevertheless, project a very unfavorable image of the practices in the criminal justice system.

Section 1983 litigation will prevail generally only when the criminal justice system, through its practitioners, has failed. If criminal justice practitioners and agencies always did their jobs properly, there would be few, if any, valid Section 1983 causes of action.

Failed Attempts to Set Liability Limits

Efforts have been made in various state legislatures to limit the amount of damages that can be recovered in liability litigation. Whether enactment of such legislation will have any effect on Section 1983 litigation is problematical, however. In *Bell v. City of Milwaukee,* 746 F.2d 1205 (7th Cir. 1984), the court affirmed over $1 million of the $1.5 million awarded by the trial court, refusing to apply the Wisconsin state law limit of $25,000 on wrongful death damages to the federal rights claims. As a separate issue in the case, the court also upheld the liability of the Milwaukee Chief of Police under 42 U.S.C. Section 1986 for his failure to adequately supervise the post-shooting investigation and to prevent the efforts of others to conceal the truth. Section 1986, a somewhat less frequently used civil rights provision, imposes liability on a person who has knowledge of a Section 1985 civil rights conspiracy and who "having power to prevent or aid in preventing" the commission of the same, neglects or refuses so to do. Also, in *Ruiz v. Estelle,* 553 F. Supp. 567 (S.D. Tex. 1982), the Federal District Court held that the state legislature could not attempt to limit the amount of attorney's fees to be paid under Section 1988 It would appear that unless Congress enacts limits of liability for federal agents (who can not be sued under Section 1983 because they do not generally act "under color" of state law, but rather can be sued directly under the Constitution (see *Bivens v. Six*

Named Unknown Agents, 403 U.S. 388, (1971)) or under the Federal Tort Claims Act), it is highly unlikely that federal courts will allow state limits to control violations of federally secured rights.

There are certainly many other developments that could be deemed to have an impact on the continued growth in the number of Section 1983 cases being filed. The point is, the times and the pressures indicate that, realistically, litigation under Section 1983 will continue unchecked for a number of years to come.

Other Developments

This is not to say that it has to be that way, however. There are also several developments and possibilities that could drastically slow down the number of cases being litigated under Section 1983.

Higher Standard of Proof Required?

In *City of Canton v. Harris,* 489 U.S. 378 (1989), the U.S. Supreme Court appeared to establish a much higher standard of proof—deliberate indifference—to render a municipality liable for inadequate training of its police officers. However, in *Burns v. Reed,* 111 S. Ct. 1934 (1991), the Court diminished the scope of absolute immunity for prosecutors.

Professionalism in Criminal Justice

Professionalism has been an elusive goal for criminal justice practitioners and operating agencies. More and more law enforcement agencies are seeking accreditation, and the training programs in many states evidence a substantial improvement over the past several years. If true professionalism can be realized, it is at least arguable that Section 1983 litigation will greatly decrease. With better qualified, better recruited, better trained, better supervised, and more highly motivated personnel, the criminal justice system should produce conduct much less likely to bring about Section 1983 litigation. In fact, Section 1983 litigation can help bring this professionalism about. By the threat of enormous damage claims and the increasing number of suits being filed, perhaps the "holders of the purse strings" will begin to allocate the necessary funds to recruit, train, and retain the quality personnel needed to "professionalize" the field. Today, the quality personnel in the field (and there is a sizable percentage of criminal justice practitioners who are truly quality personnel), have become criminal justice practitioners more by accident than by design—at least, recruitment procedures are not designed to attract the best qualified people. Perhaps the threat of lawsuits can help change those recruiting policies.

Direction of the Trends

The generally increasing prominence of civil rights litigation and the still developing nature of this area of law is reflected in the larger-than-ever number of Section 1983 and related government liability cases being filed and finding their way to the United States Supreme Court. In *Brandon v. Holt,* the Court held that "a judgment against a public servant 'in his official capacity' imposes liability on the entity that he represents." 469 U.S. 464 (1985) at 471, and in *Hafer v. Melo,* the Court said that "state officers sued for damages in their official capacity are not 'persons' for purposes of the suit because they assume the identity of the government that employs them." Slip Op., p. 5. These decisions are significant as a continuation of a line of cases that includes *Monell, Hutto v. Finney,* and *Owen.* This line of cases seems to indicate that the Supreme Court recognizes that public entities are the true bearers—both in their roles as policy determining entities and as litigators for the defense—of responsibility for civil rights violations. In addition, it would seem that these holdings are a refusal to allow such responsibility to be defeated by legal technicalities or by seeking to be shielded behind defense theories that are appropriate only regarding the responsibility of individuals. The Court is seemingly attempting to tie the amount of damages to the amount of harm done, but there are still a number of apparent inconsistencies in the Court's opinions (for example, requiring the exhaustion of state remedies in *Parratt v. Taylor* and not requiring any exhaustion of available remedies in *Patsy v. Board of Regents.* Apparent inconsistencies like these will help keep many issues unsettled and may encourage additional lawsuits.

In individual localities, when the first "big" suit is lost, additional cases will be filed rapidly. For example, when Richmond, California, lost a $3.6 million case in June, 1983 (*Roman v. City of Richmond,* 570 F. Supp. 1544 (N.D. Cal. 1983)), approximately sixty additional lawsuits against the city alleging similar deprivations were filed in less than six weeks.

There is no doubt that more and more cases will be litigated. The best advice one could give to criminal justice practitioners and agencies is to take the proactive position and attempt to prevent the lawsuits, thereby avoiding the need of trying to defend them. In short, engage in professional conduct only, and document the efforts made to improve upon conditions that lead to liability. This proactive approach seems to be the only one to make sense; playing hardball and attempting to defend the suits while doing nothing to change the conditions that brought about the suits is not only expensive, it is self-defeating. *Ruiz v. Estelle,* 553 F. Supp. 567 (S.D. Tex. 1982), resulting in an award of $1.6 million in attorneys' fees, and *Nelson v. Leeke,* #82-876-2, U.S. District Court, S.C. District (1984), which resulted in a settlement by the State of South Carolina in excess of $78 million, for example. The costs involve not only the monetary costs for damages and attorney's fees, but also the costs of public perception and a continued distrust of, and increased lack of support for, the criminal justice system and its personnel. The proactive approach will produce a more professional image and a more professional service even if it does not end all litigation. Such an image and providing such a service may well be viewed by the public as positive signs for more trust in, and more support for, the criminal justice system and its personnel; it may also be viewed by the courts as a display of good faith or even an acceptable beginning.

14 Conclusion

Born in 1871 and virtually ignored for over 90 years, Section 1983 has now come of age. Since 1978 there has literally been an explosion of litigation and the trends indicate that the numbers of cases will continue to increase, with new areas of liability being carved out and increased awards being made.

One commentator states that since *Canton v. Harris,* 1989), "lawyers have become less likely to file a claim in federal court" (Kappeler, 1993, p. 176). With regard to suits against a municipality that allege poor training, this is no doubt true, but whether Canton will have any meaningful impact on the other areas of liability remains to be seen. There have been other cases in the past that made a big splash when reported, but created few ripples. Kappeler also states that while there may be a reduction in the number of cases filed in the federal courts against the police, we may also see "the chilling effect of retarding the legal community's desire to use innovative lines of argument to plead new cases and seek exceptions to existing legal doctrine" (Kappeler, 1993, p. 176). It is true that not all Section 1983 litigation should be considered "bad" by the criminal justice community. Section 1983 has been utilized to bring about many needed systemic changes in criminal justice and has effectively identified gross misconduct on the part of criminal justice practitioners and agencies. In this way, Section 1983 has been a positive force for all those who were the subject of such misconduct and for the system itself, and thereby a positive force for society as a whole. However, because such decisions often cause the spending of locally generated revenues as ordered by the federal judiciary, reorganization of public management and, sometimes, decrease the authority of the chief administrator of an agency, this question must be asked: Is

Section 1983 litigation an effective remedy to misconduct in the criminal justice system, or is it an insidious federalism? The cases seem to show that it is some of each. Supervisors and administrators are now being held liable for the actions of their subordinates, and often the local unit of government is also held liable. These forms of liability were virtually unknown ten or fifteen years ago and have developed because of Section 1983 litigation. Such litigation has resulted in a somewhat insidious federal role in the operation of local law enforcement and corrections, but without such a federal influence it is unlikely that many of the systemic changes would have been made.

Everyone in our society has the right to expect fair treatment from all of those in the criminal justice system, and everyone needs direct access to the federal courts to remedy unjust situations caused by those practitioners. We all desire an effective but fair system staffed by professional, law-abiding personnel. Proper training and supervision costs a great deal of money, and many states and localities are suffering difficult economic times. Nevertheless, given the circumstances of the present, it would appear that communities must spend the money. The criminal justice system in our country should hire the best qualified people available, institute proper training programs, provide written policies and procedures, and provide adequate supervision. In short, the criminal justice system should professionalize in the truest sense.

If the expenditures and improvements are not made now, the cost will only be greater in the future because the costs of paying lawsuit damages and attorney's fees will be added. In addition, communities may not be allowed to solve the problems in the manner they choose, because the federal courts may dictate how it must be done (insidious federalism). Delaying these implementations is likely to be deemed as "deliberate indifference," or "gross negligence" by the courts in the future.

References

Alabama v. Pugh, 438 U.S. 781 (1978).

Allen v. City of Los Angeles, L.A. Superior Court, No. C-9837 (1975).

Alyeska Pipeline Service Co. v. Wilderness Society, 421 U.S. 240 (1975).

del Carmen, R.V. *Civil Liabilities in American Policing: A Text for Law Enforcement Personnel.* Englewood Cliffs, NJ: Brady, 1991.

Barrales v. Morris, U.S. Dist. Ct., N.D. Illinois, 1979.

Bates, R.D., R.F. Cutler & M.J. Clink (1981). *Prepared Statement on Behalf of the National Institute of Municipal Law Officers,* presented before the Subcommittee on the Constitution, Senate Committee on the Judiciary, May 6.

Beard v. Udall, 648 F.2d 1264 (9th Cir. 1981).

Bell v. City of Milwaukee, 746 F.2d 1205 (7th Cir. 1984).

Bell v. Wolfish, 441 U.S. 520 (1979).

Benny v. Pipes, 799 F.2d 489 (9th Cir. 1986), *cert. denied,* 108 S. Ct. 198 (1987).

Beverly v. Morris, 470 F.2d 1356 (5th Cir. 1972).

Billings v. Vernal City, U.S. Dist. Ct. of Utah, No. C77-0295 (1982).

Bivens v. Six Unknown Named Agents, 403 U.S. 388, 91 S. Ct. 1999 (1971).

Black v. Stephens, 662 F.2d 181 (3d Cir. 1981).

Blum v. Stenson, 465 U.S. 886, 104 S. Ct. 1541 (1984).

Block v. Rutherford, 468 U.S. 576 (1984).

Bonsignore v. City of New York, 521 F. Supp. 394 (S.D.N.Y. 1981).

Brandon v. Allen, 516 F. Supp. 1355 (W.D. Tenn. 1981).

Brandon v. Holt, 469 U.S. 464, 105 S. Ct. 873 (1985).

Branti v. Finkel, 445 U.S. 507 (1979).

Briscoe v. LaHue, 103 S. Ct. 1108 (1983).

Brawner v. Irvin, 169 F. 964 (1909).

Burkholder v. City of Los Angeles, L.A. County Superior Ct., California, October, 1982.

Burns v. Reed, 111 S. Ct. 1934 (1991).

Butz v. Economou, 438 U.S. 478 (1978).

Canton, City of v. Harris, 489 U.S. 378 (1989).

Carmelo v. Miller, 569 S.W.2d 365 (Mo. 1978).

Chapman v. Houston Welfare Rights Organization, 441 U.S. 600 (1979).

Collins v. City of Harker Heights, Texas, 112 S. Ct. 1062 (1992).

Coop v. City of South Bend, 635 F.2d 652 (7th Cir. 1981).

Copeland v. Marshall, 641 F.2d 880 (D.C. Cir. 1980).

Crime Control Digest, April 14, 1986. Fairfax, VA: Washington Crime News Service.

_____ January 6, 1992, Fairfax, VA: Washington Crime News Service.

_____ February 17, 1992, Fairfax, VA: Washington Crime News Service.

_____ September 28, 1992, Fairfax, VA: Washington Crime News Service.

_____ December 21, 1992, Fairfax, VA: Washington Crime News Service.

Crockett v. Dade County, Dade County Circuit Ct., Florida, 1976.

David v. City of Scranton, 638 F.2d 676 (3d Cir. 1980).

Davis v. Locke, 936 F.2d 1208 (11th Cir. 1991).

Davis v. Mason County, 49 CrL 1039 (1991).

Dennis v. Chang, 611 F.2d 1302 (9th Cir. 1980).

Dewell v. Lawson, 489 F.2d 877 (10th Cir. 1974).

Duncan v. Barnes, 592 F.2d 1366 (5th Cir. 1979).

Elrod v. Burns, 427 U.S. 347 (1975).

Federal Judicial Center (1980). *Recommended Procedures for Handling Prisoner Civil Rights Cases in the Federal Courts.*

Finney v. Arkansas, 505 F.2d 194 (8th Cir. 1974).

REFERENCES

Ford v. Breier, 383 F. Supp. 505 (E.D. Wis. 1974).

Ford v. Byrd, 544 F.2d 194 (5th Cir. 1976).

Gilliam v. Falbo, U.S. Dist. Ct., S.D. Ohio, April, 1982.

Hacker v. City of New York, 261 N.Y.S.2d 751 (1965).

Hamilton v. Love, 328 F. Supp. 1182 (E.D. Ark. 1971).

Haring v. Prosise, 103 S. Ct. 2368 (1983).

Harlow v. Fitzgerald, 102 S. Ct. 2727 (1982).

Haygood v. City of Detroit, Wayne County Circuit Ct., Michigan, No. 77-728013 NO, December 29, 1980.

Helling v. McKinney, No. 91-1958, 1/18/93, 53 CrL 2230.

Hendrickson v. Branstad, 934 F.2d 158 (8th Cir. 1991).

Hensley v. Eckerhart, 103 S. Ct. 1933 (1983).

Herbert v. City of Texas City, U.S. Dist. Ct., S.D. Texas, 1981.

Hudson v. McMillian, 503 U.S. 1 (1992), Slip Opinion, 2/25/92.

Hudson v. Palmer, 468 U.S. 517 (1984).

Hutto v. Finney, 437 U.S. 687 (1978).

Imbler v. Pachtman, 424 U.S. 409, 96 S. Ct. 984 (1976).

Jennings v. City of Detroit, Wayne County Circuit Ct., Michigan, August, 1979.

Johnson v. Georgia Highway Express, Inc., 488 F.2d 714 (5th Cir. 1974).

Kappeler, V.E. (1993). *Critical Issues in Police Civil Liability*, Prospect Heights, IL: Waveland Press, Inc.

Kelley v. Johnson, 96 S. Ct. 1440 (1976).

Keffler v. Meer, 936 F.2d 981 (7th Cir. 1991).

Leonard v. City of Columbus, 705 F.2d 1299 (11th Cir. 1983).

Liability Reporter, Number 229, January 1992. Chicago, IL: AELE.

_____ Number 239, November 1992. Chicago, IL: AELE.

Lloyd, A. (1983). *Money Damages in Police Misconduct Cases: A Compilation of Jury Awards and Settlements.* New York, NY: Clark Boardman Company, Ltd.

Lund, L., Personal communication, March, 1982.

Maine v. Thiboutot, 448 U.S. 1, 100 S. Ct. 2502 (1980).

Mancini v. Lester, 630 F.2d 990 (3d Cir. 1980).

Martinez v. California, 444 U.S. 277 (1980).

Marusa v. District of Columbia, 484 F.2d 828 (D.C. Cir. 1973).

Massachusetts Fair Share v. O'Keefe, 476 F. Supp. 294 (D. Mass. 1979).

McClelland v. Facteau, 610 F.2d 693 (10th Cir. 1979).

McNamara v. Moody, 606 F.2d 621 (5th Cir. 1979).

Mee v. Ortega, 51 CrL 1353, 6/18/92.

Monell v. Dept. of Social Services, 436 U.S. 658, 98 S. Ct. 2018 (1978).

Monroe v. Pape, 365 U.S. 167, 81 S. Ct. 473 (1961).

Moon v. Winfield, 383 F. Supp. 31 (N.D. Ill. 1974).

Motley v. McCallum, Wayne County, Michigan, No. 79-719-897-NO, January, 1982.

Murray v. City of Chicago, 634 F.2d 365 (7th Cir. 1980).

Murray v. Murphy, 441 F. Supp. 120 (E.D. Pa. 1977).

N.C.W. (1985). "Seeking Solutions on Liability Insurance." *Nation's Cities Weekly* (Nov. 25). Washington, DC: National League of Cities.

Nelson v. Leeke, U.S. Dist. Ct, SC Dist., No. 82-876-2, 1984.

Newport, City of v. Fact Concerts, Inc., 101 S. Ct. 2748 (1981).

New York v. Quarles, 104 S. Ct. 2626 (1984).

Nix v. Williams, 104 S. Ct. 2501 (1984).

O'Connor v. Donaldson, 422 U.S. 563 (1975).

Executive Assistant to the Commissioner for Legal Settlements and Compliance. *First Quarterly Compliance Report (Nelson v. Leeke),* South Carolina Department of Corrections, Columbia, SC, April 8, 1985.

Oklahoma City v. Tuttle, 105 S. Ct. 2427 (1985).

Owen v. City of Independence, 455 U.S. 622, 100 S. Ct. 1398 (1980).

Owens v. Haas, 601 F.2d 1242 (2d Cir.), *cert. denied,* 100 S. Ct. 483 (1979).

Parratt v. Taylor, 101 S. Ct. 1908 (1981).

Parrish v. Luckie, 963 F.2d 201 (8th Cir. 1992).

Parsons v. Pfeiffer, U.S. Dist. Ct., N.D. Illinois, 1975.

Patsy v. Board of Regents, 102 S. Ct. 2557 (1982).

Pembaur v. City of Cincinnati, 475 U.S. 469 (1986).

REFERENCES

Pennsylvania v. Porter, 659 F.2d 306 (3d Cir. 1981), *cert. denied,* 102 S. Ct. 3509 (1982).

Peters v. Bellinger, 159 N.E.2d 528 (Ill. App. 1959).

Pierson v. Ray, 386 U.S. 547, 87 S. Ct. 1213 (1967).

Police Misconduct and Civil Rights, Law Report, Vol. 2, No. 6, November-December, 1987. New York, New York: Clark Boardman.

_____ Vol. 3, No.15, May-June, 1992. New York, New York: Clark Boardman.

Popow v. City of Margate, 476 F. Supp. 1237 (D.N.J. 1979).

Powe v. City of Chicago, 664 F.2d 639 (7th Cir. 1981).

Prior v. Woods, U.S. Dist. Ct., E.D. Mich., October, 1981.

Procunier v. Navarette, 434 U.S. 555 (1978).

Pulliam v. Allen, 466 U.S. 522 (1984).

Rhodes v. City of Wichita, 516 F. Supp. 501 (D. Kan. 1981).

Riddell v. National Democratic Party, 624 F.2d 539 (5th Cir. 1980).

Rizzo v. Goode, 423 U.S. 362, 96 S. Ct. 598 (1976).

Roe v. Wade, 410 U.S. 113 (1973).

Ruiz v. Estelle, 553 F. Supp. 567 (S.D. Tex. 1982).

Ryer v. Sweeny, L.A. County Superior Ct., California, June, 1973.

Saddlewhite v. City of Los Angeles, (Citation Unknown, 1982 Settlement).

Sager v. City of Woodlawn Park, 543 F. Supp. 282 (D. Colo. 1982).

Saldana v. Garza, 32 CrL 2022 (1982).

Salenas v. Breier, 517 F. Supp. 1272 (E.D. Wis. 1981).

Sawyer v. Humphries, Md. Ct. App., No-44-1990, 3/22/91, 49 CrL 1017.

Scheuer v. Rhodes, 416 U.S. 232 (1974).

Screws v. United States, 325 U.S. 91 (1945).

Sellars v. Procunier, 641 F.2d 1295 (9th Cir.), *cert. denied,* 454 U.S. 1102 (1981).

Silver, I. (1991). *Police Civil Liability.* New York, NY: Matthew Bender.

Slaughterhouse Cases, 83 U.S. (16 Wall.) 36 (1873).

Slavin v. Currey, 574 F.2d 1256 (5th Cir. 1978).

Smith v. Wade, 103 S. Ct. 1625 (1983).

Stengel v. Belcher, 522 F.2d 438 (6th Cir. 1975).

Stump v. Sparkman, 435 U.S. 349 (1978).

Supreme Court of Virginia v. Consumers Union, 446 U.S. 719 (1980).

Swope v. Bratton, 541 F. Supp. 99 (W.D. Ark. 1982).

Taken Alive v. Litzau, 551 F.2d 196 (8th Cir. 1977).

Tenny v. Brandhove, 341 U.S. 367 (1951).

Title 42 United States Code, Section 1983.

Title 42 United States Code, Section 1988.

Tuttle v. Oklahoma City, 728 F.2d 456 (10th Cir. 1984).

United States v. Classic, 313 U.S. 299, 61 S. Ct. 1031 (1941).

United States v. Leon, 104 S. Ct. 3405 (1984).

Universal Amusement Co. v. Hofheinz, 646 F.2d 996 (5th Cir. 1981).

Venegas v. Mitchell, 495 U.S. 82 (1990).

Webster v. City of Houston, 689 F.2d 1220 (5th Cir. 1982).

Whiteley v. Warden, 401 U.S. 560 (1971).

Will v. Michigan Department of State Police, 491 U.S. 58 (1989).

William v. Alioto, 625 F.2d 845 (9th Cir. 1980).

Williams v. Anderson, 559 F.2d 923 (10th Cir. 1979).

Wood v. Strickland, 420 U.S. 308, 85 S. Ct. 992 (1975).

Youngberg v. Romero, 102 S. Ct. 2452 (1982).

Zarcone v. Perry, 581 F.2d 1039 (2d Cir. 1978).

Zimmerman, C. (1990). "Court Comparisons of Compensatory Damage Awards: A Critique and a Re-Compilation of Damage Awards in the Federal Courts." *Police Misconduct and Civil Rights Law Report*, Vol. 3, No. 6, November-December.

Index

Alabama v. Pugh, 27
Allen v. City of Los Angeles, 57
Alyeska Pipeline Service Co. v. Wilderness Society, 21, 22
American rule, 21
Attorney's fees, 67

Barrales v. Morris, 44
Beard v. Udall, 51
Bell v. City of Milwaukee, 45, 92
Bell v. Wolfish, 38
Benny v. Pipes, 35
Beverly v. Morris, 59
Billings v. Vernal City, 61, 84
Bivens v. Six Unknown Named Agents, 92-93
Black v. Stephens, 68-70
Blum v. Stenson, 24
Block v. Rutherford, 38
Bonsignore v. City of New York, 58
Brandon v. Allen, 56, 66, 67, 82
Brandon v. Holt, 58, 67, 94
Branti v. Finkel, 74-76
Briscoe v. LaHue, 42, 53
Brawner v. Irvin, 8
Burkholder v. City of Los Angeles, 44
Burns v. Reed, 52, 93
Butz v. Economou, 49

Canton, City of v. Harris, 17, 59, 60, 85, 93, 97

Carmelo v. Miller, 46
Chapman v. Houston Welfare Rights Organization, 25
City of Oklahoma City v. Tuttle, 61, 62
Civil Rights Attorney's Fees Award Act of 1976,
    See Title 42 U.S.C. Section 1988
Class action, 17
Collins v. City of Harker Heights, 72
Constitutional torts, 3
Coop v. City of South Bend, 23
Copeland v. Marshall, 23
Crime, definition, 1
Crime vs. tort, major differences, 1, 2
Crockett v. Dade County, 44

David v. City of Scranton, 23
Davis v. Little, 43-44
Davis v. Locke, 24
Davis v. Mason County, 59
Defenses, 79 *et seq.*
    an "acceptable beginning," 81
    good faith test, 81
    invalid, 82, 83
    qualified immunity, 79, 80
    valid authority, 82
Dennis v. Chang, 19
Dewell v. Lawson, 37, 58, 59
Domashewsky v. Sierociuk, 47, 82
Duncan v. Barnes, 40

Elrod v. Burns, 74
Exclusionary rule, 89

Finney v. Arkansas, 27, 82
Ford v. Breier, 57, 81, 86
Ford v. Byrd, 30

Gilliam v. Falbo, 42
Good faith test, 81
Graddstaff v. City of Borger, 45
Gutierrez-Rodriguez v. Cartagena, 43

Hacker v. City of New York, 46
Hafer v. Melo, 65, 67, 94
Hall v. Ochs, 44
Hamilton v. Love, 82
Haring v. Prosise, 42
Harlow v. Fitzgerald, 81
Haygood v. City of Detroit, 43
Helling v. McKinney, 38
Hendrickson v. Branstad, 24
Hensley v. Eckerhart, 23
Herbert v. City of Texas City, 43
Herrera v. Valentine, 44
Hudson v. McMillian, 35
Hudson v. Palmer, 38
Hutto v. Finney, 27, 83, 94

Imbler v. Pachtman, 42, 51
Intentional torts, 3
Intentional state torts, 6
Invalid defenses, 82-83

Jennings v. City of Detroit, 43
Jones v. City of Santa Monica, 43
Johnson v. Georgia Highway Express, Inc., 19-21, 24
Judges, 49

Kelley v. Johnson, 73
Ku Klux Klan Act of 1871, 8-9

Languirand v. Hayden, 43
Lawsuit prevention, 83
    documentation, 85
    know the law, 83
    policies and procedures, 83-84
    supervision, 84-85
    training, 84
Leffler v. Meer, 24
Legislators, 53
Leonard v. City of Columbus, 74

Maine v. Thiboutot, 16-30
Mancini v. Lester, 51
Martinez v. California, 52, 53
Marusa v. District of Columbia, 58, 84
Massachusettes Fair Share v. O'Keefe, 23
McClelland v. Facteau, 56, 65-67
McNamara v. Moody, 23, 36, 37, 68
Mee v. Ortega, 53
Miranda v. Arizona, 89
Monell v. Department of Social Services, 12, 13, 14, 16, 17, 26, 28, 30, 94
    importance of, 13-14
Monroe v. Pape, 11, 12, 14, 28, 30, 40, 55, 56, 63, 64, 79, 82
Moon v. Winfield, 57
Moses v. City of Chicago, 45
Motley v. McCallum, 42
Murray v. City of Chicago, 41
Murray v. Murphy, 57

Negligence, 3
    as a cause of action under § 1983, 55 *et seq.*
    as a state tort, 6
    degrees of and extent of damages, 55-56
Nelson v. Leeke, 36, 37, 95
Newport, City of v. Fact Concerts, Inc., 17
New York v. Quarles, 89
Nix v. Williams, 89

O'Connor v. Donaldson, 80
Oklahoma City v. Tuttle, 77

INDEX

Owen v. City of Independence, 14, 15, 16, 30, 76, 94
Owens v. Haas, 34, 35, 56, 58, 82

Parole officials, 52
Parratt v. Taylor, 56, 62, 63, 64, 94
Parrish v. Luckie, 58
Parsons v. Pfeiffer, 43
Patsy v. Board of Regents, 76, 77, 94
Pembaur v. City of Cincinnati, 17
Pennsylvania v. Porter, 17
Personal liability—
    administrators and supervisors, 65 *et seq.*
    elements of lawsuit, 67-68
Personnel issues under § 1983, 71 *et seq.*
    discipline/firing, 73
    due process requirements, 76
    exhaustion of administrative remedies, 76
    failure to warn, 72
    non-hire, 72
    non-promotion, 72
Peters v. Bellinger, 57
Pierson v. Ray, 49, 50, 79
Popow v. City of Margate, 60
Powe v. City of Chicago, 41, 42
Prior v. Woods, 44
Proactive principles, 85
    evaluation, 85
    implementation, 86
    management and money, 85
    master plan, 86
    prioritize, 86
Procunier v. Navarette, 81
Prosecutors, 51-52
Pulliam v. Allen, 51

Respondeat superior, 28
Rhodes v. City of Wichita, 17, 28, 30
Riddell v. National Democratic Party, 19
Rizzo v. Goode, 29
Roe v. Wade, 26
Roman v. City of Richmond, 45, 94

Ruiz v. Estelle, 22, 92, 95
Ryer v. Sweeny, 44

Saddlewhite v. City of Los Angeles, 43
Sager v. City of Woodlawn Park, 61, 84
Saldana v. Garza, 41
Salinas v. Breier, 81
Sawyer v. Humphries, 47
Scher v. Engelke, 91
Scheuer v. Rhodes, 80
Screws v. United States, 9
Sellars v. Procunier, 52
Slaughterhouse Cases, 8
Smith v. Wade, 33, 34, 60
Stengel v. Belcher, 46, 47, 57
Stump v. Sparkman, 50
Supreme Court of Virginia v. Consumers Union, 49, 53
Swann v. City of Goldsboro, 45
Swope v. Bratton, 73

Taken Alive v. Litzau, 29
Tenny v. Brandhove, 53
Title 42 United States Code, Section 1983—
    actions in corrections, 33 *et seq.*
        cruel and unusual punishment, 37
        management issues, 38
        medical care, 37
        overcrowded prisons, 36
        physical abuse, 33
        use of the mail, 36
        visitation, 36
    actions in law enforcement, 39 *et seq.*
        false arrest, 41
        false testimony, 42
        illegal search and seizure, 39, 40
        off-duty activities, 45, 46
        police brutality, 42, 43, 44
        wrongful death actions, 44, 45
    cause of action, 25 *et seq.*
    current status, 9
    expansion of, 12
    history of, 8, 9

magnitude of litigation, 30, 31, 32
negligence as cause of action, 55
    et seq.
  negligent assignment, 57
  negligent direction, 57
  negligent entrustment, 57
  negligent hiring, 57
  negligent retention, 57
  negligent supervision, 58
  negligent training, 58
other actions, 49 *et seq.*
  judges, 49
  legislators, 53
  parole officials, 52
  prosecutors, 51-52
  witnesses, 53
personnel issues, 71 *et seq.*
  exhaustion of administrative
      remedies, 76
  discipline/firing, 73
  non-hire, 72
  non-promotion, 72
resuscitation of, 11 *et seq.*
statutory language, 7
under "color of state law," 27, 28
who can be sued, 26, 27
who can sue, 25, 26
Title 42 United States Code,
  Section 1988—
  American rule, 21
  attorney's fees for the
      defendant, 23
  impact of, 22
  statutory language, 19
Tort—
  categories of, 2-3
  constitutional torts, 3
  definition, 1
  intentional torts, 3
  intentional state tort, 6
  negligence, 3
  negligent state tort, 6
  versus crime, 1
Trends in liability litigation, 89 *et seq.*
  abuses continue, 91
  continued changes, 90
  direction of trends, 94
  growing weight of precedent,
      91
  lawyers more familiar, 90
  population migration, 90

United States v. Classic, 9, 28
United States v. Leon, 89
*Universal Amusement Co. v.
    Hofheinz*, 27
Urseth v. City of Dayton, 45

Venegas v. Mitchell, 24

Whiteley v. Warden, 85
*Will v. Michigan Department of
    State Police*, 27
William v. Alioto, 23
Williams v. Anderson, 29
Witnesses, 53
Wood v. Strickland, 80, 81

Youngberg v. Romero, 80

Zarcone v. Perry, 50, 51